STRANGE FIRE

To Debbie,

Many Continued Blessings!

Pastor Keith D. Dickens
09/19/21

STRANGE FIRE

Worship in the African American Church

J. Wendell Mapson, Jr.
Xulon Press

Xulon Press
2301 Lucien Way #415
Maitland, FL 32751
407.339.4217
www.xulonpress.com

© 2017 by J. Wendell Mapson, Jr.

All rights reserved solely by the author. The author guarantees all contents are original and do not infringe upon the legal rights of any other person or work. No part of this book may be reproduced in any form without the permission of the author. The views expressed in this book are not necessarily those of the publisher.

Scripture quotations taken from the King James Version (KJV) – *public domain*.

Scripture quotations taken from the New King James Version (NKJV). Copyright © 1982 by Thomas Nelson, Inc. Used by permission. All rights reserved.

Scripture quotations taken from the Holy Bible, New International Version (NIV). Copyright © 1973, 1978, 1984, 2011 by Biblica, Inc.™. Used by permission. All rights reserved.

Printed in the United States of America.

ISBN-13: 9781498498432

This book is dedicated to my wife,
Shirley
To our three sons,
Keith, Brian, and Jesse III,
and to the loving people of
the Monumental Baptist Church
Philadelphia, Pennsylvania

Contents

Foreword
Page - ix

Chapter One
Strange Fire
Page - 1

Chapter Two
And the House Was Filled with Smoke
Page - 17

Chapter Three
A New Song
Page - 31

Chapter Four
An Uncertain Sound
Page - 47

Chapter Five
The Romance of Worship
Page - 65

Chapter Six
No Night There
Page - 83

Chapter Seven
A Day in Thy Courts
Page - 99

FOREWORD

The Hampton University Ministers' Conference is the forum for great and timeless ideas. Those asked to share that stage must speak with an understanding of the present, and appreciation for the past, and a keen awareness of what is lurking on the horizon. Dr. J. Wendell Mapson understood that challenge when he took the stage at the conference and opened our eyes to the changing patterns that are impinging upon us today and reshaping the church as we know it. He entitled those presentations, *Strange Fire,* and called us to attention as to what is genuine worship and what the Lord requires when we *enter His gates with thanksgiving and His courts with praise.* Seldom is one given a two-year platform to present on a topic, but Dr. Mapson's first round of presentations left the audience hungry for more and he was invited back to take us deeper. Every aspect of our worship experience he opened for our review and reflection. I remember sitting in that massive room as he called us to rethink what we know as worship and the place it holds in our lives, and promised God I would never allow worship to seek any goal but that of glorifying God.

Dr. Mapson's words then are still speaking now. In a time when many church leaders are wrestling with the new realities of the 21st century, Dr. Mapson reissues this opus to give us direction for this critical challenge. His presentations give us a theological framework for understanding the purpose, power, and persuasiveness of worship. That thinking is sometimes lost in an effort to get an effect, but Dr. Mapson calls us to return to the foundations upon which worship is offered and to see God bless us with the glory of God's presence.

Few know that Dr. Mapson is an accomplished musician. Some of us have been listening for years to his awesome renditions of the music of our people. Many a Saturday night, as a way of preparing myself for worship, I sat listening to him play the great hymns of the faith. He is a lover of worship and it comes through every word, phrase, and sentence of this volume. He does not want us to miss the opportunity to glorify God or to experience the enrapturing presence of God. Each chapter drips with his appreciation for the culture that taught him this respect for worship and that nurtured him as he grew closer to God. That is his aim. He wants us closer to God; he wants us to be able to move the rocks that the times are putting on the worship path, so that we can ride straight into the presence of God. From morning worship to funeral services, he never lets us forget the sheer majesty of our worship of the true and living God.

Read each page and take time to fully digest what he is saying. I am so glad he reissued this seminal work so that this generation may benefit from these insights. Hampton preachers left the room shouting and crying, and now the words that opened their hearts and minds are made available to you. May they have so deep an impression upon you as well.

Bishop Walter S. Thomas, Pastor
New Psalmist Baptist Church
Baltimore, Maryland

INTRODUCTION

My love for the sacred music of the black church began in my formative years, first through my mother, who earlier in her own life, sang in the church choir and played the piano for her own enjoyment and inspiration. With somewhat faded memory, I can still see her at the piano in our living room of my childhood home, where often in the quiet evening hours she played the great hymns of the church. Two of her favorites, *Thy Way, O Lord, Not Mine*, and *A Prayer in One Accord,* found in the old Baptist Standard Hymnal, unfortunately, are rarely if ever used today in most of our churches. I can never remember a time when there wasn't a piano in the home of my youth, and through the years, a piano has been a part of the furnishings in my home. Every now and then, but not often enough, I sit at the piano and play those hymnic melodies for my own devotional enjoyment.

I have often stated that I was raised in the north, but in a southern home. Though my parents had moved from the South, they carried with them the southern faith, values, culture and cuisine of their generation. Two things valued in our home were education and music. My father had left Florida in 1947 to answer the call to become pastor of Mt. Calvary Missionary Baptist Church, Newark, NJ. where we joined countless others who left the segregated South for a better life. It is estimated that from the end of World War I to 1960 as many as 7 million blacks left the South for northern and midwestern cities searching for job opportunities and freedoms denied them in the Jim Crow South. Though my father was not a singing preacher, there was music in his voice, music that found its genesis in the black preaching tradition honed in the backwoods of Alabama, the ancestral home state of both my father and mother. Through the years I have often wondered why God chose to block my inheritance of my father's great preaching style and gift, while at the same time grateful for what gifts He has given to me, especially the gift of His amazing and undeserved grace. Our parents insisted that we (my two younger sisters and brother) take piano lessons, which we did, since we had no choice.

Early on I was attracted to the organ in my father's church, and learned to play from our church's Minister of Music, who never charged for a lesson. I grew up playing for BTU (Baptist Training Union), and later for Sunday School and the Junior and Young Adult Choirs. As a college student, I played for the A. Franklin Fisher Choir in the West Hunter St. Baptist Church, Atlanta, GA., pastored by Rev. Ralph David Abernathy, a close friend and associate of Dr. Martin Luther King, Jr. Other than my father, Rev. Abernathy became for me a beloved mentor and father in ministry. He, and his wife Juanita, were extremely kind to me during my years at Morehouse, and though he has since gone to be with the Lord, Mrs. Abernathy remains a close and dear friend to this day.

All of the material accept the final chapter in this book was originally presented as lectures in both 1994 and 1995, during the 80th and 81st annual gatherings of the Hampton University Ministers' Conference and Choir and Organists' Guild, held on the campus of historic Hampton University, Hampton, VA. The university (then called Hampton Institute) was founded in 1868 to educate ex-slaves recently emancipated from the long, dark night of slavery, ironically on land that was once a plantation. It was the first conference held in the then newly

Introduction

opened convocation center, and I was scheduled to give the very first lecture in the new auditorium. The audience for the Conference and these lectures is primarily pastors and ministers, although many laypersons attend as well.

Initially, I wrestled with whether or not to put, again in print, lectures presented over two decades ago, since both the world and the church have dramatically changed, even in the short span of twenty years, and we have since moved into a new century. In the mid 1990s, when these lectures were first presented, technology was just gaining its footing, and very soon cell phones, the Internet, and other electronic devices were poised to burst on the scene. I remember the trustees in our church engaging in a long discussion about whether or not to buy this new thing called a fax machine. Then, there was no Facebook or Instagram, and when the preacher invited the congregants to open their Bibles to a passage of scripture, worshippers actually opened a book and not an "app" on a smartphone. Then, the prosperity gospel, which has attracted so many of the faithful with its false and misleading claims, was in its infancy, and keyboards were rarely seen among musical instruments in the sanctuary. In many churches today, keyboards have replaced pianos as instruments of choice, and hymnals are almost obsolete, as well as the singing of hymns, which contain our theology. In the age of technology in many of our churches, the words of songs and scripture are scrolled on large monitors in the sanctuary. In fact, many of the hymns quoted in these lectures are rarely sung today in many, if not most of our churches.

However, in spite of my own reservations, and because many over the years have requested a reprinting of these lectures, I yielded, in hopes that these messages, though perhaps dated by time, are valuable enough to speak to the Church in this present age. The reader must determine whether or not my effort has been worthwhile. It is my belief that the word of God, whether in sermonic or lecture form, is timeless, because we believe and preach a timeless Gospel, the faith *that was once, for all entrusted to the saints* (Jude 1:3). The Spirit can breathe new life into the print on the worn and tattered pages of yesteryear. Even in my own devotional moments, I continue to read printed sermons of the great preachers of long ago, and marvel at how the Holy Spirit yet breathes anew into the printed page, and my thirst is quenched and my soul refreshed.

In preparing these lectures when first delivered, I was determined to be faithful to my assignment, which was to lecture, not preach. I think that preachers, including myself, should not only know, but also respect the difference. However, there is a point in the African-American religious experience when lecture and sermon merge, and lecture becomes *sermonic*. Though I plead guilty to sometimes crossing the line, I do what many preachers I know have done, which is to put all the blame on the Holy Spirit and the prompting of the congregation. Across the years, particularly in the years immediately following the presentation of these messages, I have been asked to repeat them, and each time I have declined. Though I am aware of the saying that if a sermon is not worth preaching a second time, it wasn't worth preaching the first time, I have never attempted to *re-lecture* or *re-preach* these messages in spite of requests to do so, for there is no way to recapture such moments, once passed. If those moments in Hampton's convocation center live, they must live on in my own memory and in the hearts and minds of the original hearers, many of whom are now with the Lord. In reading over these lectures after these many years, there were, to me, obvious places where rewording and re-editing seemed appropriate and necessary. Even so, I have tried to remain faithful to the original form and content.

At the center of these lectures is the question of how can we give God more empowering worship and a more excellent song, for worship remains, and rightly so, at the center of the church's life and distinguishes us from any other body of people on the

Introduction

face of the earth. I still believe–and even more so today than in the past–as I look across the landscape of the modern-day church, that in too many instances, Sunday morning entertainment has replaced authentic worship, and we are singing songs high in volume, but low in theological soundness and Biblical integrity. Our songs, as our sermons, ought to at least tell the truth about God. May we always seek to give God our best, since He gave to us His best–His Son and our Savior, Jesus Christ. God deserves a greater offering than just *strange* fire.

One final note. On one of the walls in the rear of our sanctuary in the Monumental Baptist Church, where I have been pastor for almost 30 years, is a plaque with the names of families in our church who participated in an effort I led in recent years to purchase new pews. As far as we know, the new pews are the first since the original pews were installed when the church was built by a United Church of Christ congregation, during the second decade of the 20th century. The new pews, along with other sanctuary furnishings, were dedicated in March 2013. Etched at the bottom of the plaque are words quoted from the book of Nehemiah: *We will not neglect the house of our God* (10:39). To this end, I have added another chapter to *Strange Fire*, one not a part of the original six lectures. It contains additional material taken from an aging manuscript written by me a few years ago, but never used. I came across it not long ago gathering dust, and thought some of the material worth updating and presenting in this book as closing thoughts. In it, I take a deeper look at the space in which we worship God and how particularities within this sacred space can aid in our understanding of this awesome God we worship and serve. I have entitled this final offering, taken from Psalm 84, *A Day in Thy Courts*.

Jesse Wendell Mapson, Jr
January 2017

And yet I show you a more excellent way . . .
(1 Cor. 12:31b)

ACKNOWLEDGMENTS

I am forever grateful to my father, the Rev. J. Wendell Mapson, Sr., now home with the Lord, and my mother, Georgia T. Mapson, who yet lives at the blessed age of 94, for providing for me a home where Christ was present, and where my faith in Him was both birthed and nurtured; and for loving and supportive siblings, my younger sisters Zaundria and Paulette, and my brother Charles.

To the members of the Mt. Calvary Missionary Baptist Church, Newark, NJ, where I was baptized, licensed to preach, married, and ordained into the Gospel ministry, and where the foundation of my faith was laid, though most of those who influenced my early life have already fallen asleep, I will forever cherish my beginnings. It was in Mt. Calvary, a northern church steeped in southern culture and traditions, where I first heard the preaching of the Gospel from the heart and tongue of my father, gifted with a black preaching style honed in the deep woods of Alabama; and first witnessed the singing of the great hymns, anthems, gospel songs, spirituals, and meter hymns of our faith tradition. I can still hear those old deacons "moaning" those soulful tunes during Communion on 1st Sunday evenings.

To the Union Baptist Church, Elizabeth, NJ–my first pastorate–words cannot express my sincere gratitude. This congregation that accepted and loved me in the early morning of my ministry at the tender and inexperienced age of twenty-three. These were a people who were patient with me as I sought to discover my own preaching voice, and sharpen what God had already placed in my head and heart. It was a wonderful eighteen-year journey and a heart-wrenching separation when God called me to another field of ministerial labor in the *City of Brotherly Love*.

To the people of the Monumental Baptist Church, Philadelphia, an historic congregation (organized in 1826) I have now been privileged to lead and serve for almost 30 years, I say, "Thank you!" Not only have you provided me the opportunity to preach and to pastor unencumbered and without restraint, you have allowed me the freedom to minister and travel far beyond the corner of 50th and Locust Sts. It is a wonderful experience when, over the span of many years, love deepens between a pastor and people. Still my greatest joy is standing before you on Sunday morning with a word from the Lord.

I offer expressions of appreciation to Tanya Hoard for graciously retyping and offering editorial suggestions and for her valuable assistance in helping to bring this project to fruition. And to Jesse Mapson III, Director of Special Projects and Janeen Hayes, Executive Director, both on the staff at Monumental, for valuable assistance in the promotion of this book. I am grateful to Rev. D. Keith Owens, pastor of Salem Baptist Church, Jersey City, NJ, and a former executive with the American Baptist Churches, for his valuable insight, comments and editorial suggestions. I am grateful to the 1994-5 leadership of the Hampton University Ministers' Conference for granting to me the opportunity to stand on such a large and prominent platform, where over many decades so many of the giants of church and academy have stood. Thanks to Bishop Walter Scott Thomas, pastor of the New Psalmist Baptist Church, Baltimore, MD, and longtime friend, who consented

Acknowledgments

to write the foreword for this book, and who was instrumental in opening the door for me to deliver these lectures.

Last, but not least, I am grateful to Shirley, my beloved and adored wife of almost 30 years, for her limitless devotion, support, gentle critiques when necessary, and for sharing life and love with me; and for our three sons, Keith, Brian, and Jesse III, who was in a stroller at four years of age when the first three of these lectures were delivered.

. . . I thank Christ Jesus our Lord who has enabled me, because He counted me faithful, putting me into the ministry (1 Timothy 1:12).

Jesse Wendell Mapson, Jr.

Chapter One

STRANGE FIRE

We gather here today on this hallowed ground where our ancestors, fresh from the long, dark night of slavery, started a school (Hampton Institute) to train black boys and girls how to survive in a hostile world trying to beat them into the ground.

With nothing more than God and a song, they made their way through the jungle of unfulfilled dreams and hope deferred. Now, over a century later, we gather here today because they left us a legacy that must be preserved, but not deified; honored, but not worshipped; respected, but not idolized. I believe that our purpose for being here is to examine and reexamine what we offer God, who speaks to us in every age and in every situation.

As we approach the beginning of a new century, indeed a new millennium, the church stands at a crossroad. We are being challenged as never before for the hearts and minds of men and women, boys and girls. Not only is this assault being leveled by the forces of a secular society whose god is not our God, but also the real assault is coming from forces wearing religious garments. They look like us; they talk religious talk; they sing religious songs; they engage in religious exercise; and they worship in buildings that look like churches. But subtly, quietly, and discretely, they are pulling away the sons and daughters, and the grandsons, and granddaughters of those who once held fast to the faith of our fathers and mothers.

The church is being deserted by Aunt Jane's grandchildren; and if they go to church at all, their Volvos, Audis and Benzs are parked in the parking lots of new age *Word* churches. These churches are desegregated, but not necessarily integrated. The members call themselves, *born-again Christians*, even though the term is redundant. If you are a Christian, you are born again. These churches preach a gospel of conservatism, and abound with misleading slogans such as, *name it and claim it*, and *let go and let God*. Theologically, they put more weight on being successful than being faithful. Their sermons are more priestly, than prophetic. They are pastored by shepherds who can't relate to a history of pain and disenfranchisement.

In their approach to God, the singing of spirituals is an embarrassment, a reminder of a past they are admonished to forget, or encouraged to gloss over as if slavery never happened. They pat us on the head and tell us that slavery was not so bad, and that if you keep working hard, you will overcome someday. And the so-called gospel songs they sing do not know whether the *He* in the song is God, or a lover. That's because the music wants to play well on both sides of the fence: the religious side and the secular side.

I submit to you today that we need to re-examine what we offer God, especially when it comes to worship, which is the primary reason we were created and formed from the earth's dust by a loving God. Our ancestors took the words of Charles Wesley, and sang:

Oh, for a heart to praise my God; a heart from sin set free.
A heart that's sprinkled with the blood, so freely shed for me.

God made us to glorify Him. The Westminster confession says it best: "What is the chief end of man?" The answer is "... to glorify God and enjoy Him forever." In this series of lectures, I shall attempt to do several things.

First, I shall attempt to define worship and raise issues concerning the nature and importance of worship in the life of the church. Attention will be given to worship in general, but the African-American worship experience in particular. I shall attempt to get us to look critically at the present state of worship and offer suggestions to improve worship in the church.

Second, I will attempt to look closely at those who have been given the primary responsibility of leading worship. This includes the pastor, the musician, and the choir member. What are their respective roles in the enhancement of the worship of God? Some attention will be given to the place of instruments, which may accompany worship.

Finally, as we stand poised to enter a new century, I will examine how can we take the best of our heritage and blend it with the needs and concerns of a new day, an "MTV" (Music Television) age? How does the worship of God embrace the contemporary, yet maintain its integrity? How can we sing a new song?

This first lecture is entitled, *Strange Fire*. It is inspired by a passage of scripture found in the book of Leviticus, a book often collecting the dust of neglect on the part of the average modern Christian. In the book of Leviticus, we find a worshipping congregation led by Moses. Aaron and his sons, who were anointed as priests, presided over the offering of sacrifices unto the Lord. There was the sin offering, the meat offering, and the peace offering, etc. The tenth chapter records that two sons of Aaron, Nadab and Abihu, offered *strange fire* before the Lord, which he had commanded them not to do. The text says:

And Nadab and Abihu, the sons of Aaron, took either of them his censer, and put fire therein, and put incense thereon, and offered strange fire before the LORD, which he commanded them not (Lev. 10:1).

The next verse says:

So, fire went out from the LORD, and devoured them, and they died before the LORD (Lev. 10:2).

There are problems within the text. First of all, what a harsh penalty for offering *strange fire*. Did the punishment fit the crime? Second, what did they do wrong? They seemed to have gone by the book. They took their censers, which were shovel-like devices used to carry live coals and to burn incense. They put fire and incense on them, and made their offering just as they had done at earlier times. Was the fault in following procedure? Or, was the fault in attitude? Was the problem external or internal? What we do know is that what they had offered was not just fire; it was *strange fire*. For that, they died before the Lord.

It seems to me that whatever else the text implies, it is clear that worship is to be taken seriously. I recognize the controversial nature of this statement, but it is my belief that worship is the most important activity in which we engage as Christians. I know that the true impact of our faith is felt, not when the church is gathered, but when the church is scattered. Yet it is what happens in the gathering of God's people that affects what happens in the scattering of God's people. We worship God in order to serve God. We do not serve in order to worship, though when we serve we also worship.

In the sixties, during the Civil Rights Movement, some northern students, who went south to join the marches and the protests, could not understand why our people gathered first in rural frame churches on hot summer nights, using fans donated by the local undertaker, where they sang and prayed and testified and preached and then marched.

They did not understand that it was through worship and praise that black people were given power, courage, fortitude, and faith. It was worship that empowered God's dispossessed and gave them strength for the perilous journey. It was the assurance of divine presence that fueled the fires of social justice. What we do in the church building has a direct relationship to what we do outside the church building. Work without worship becomes nothing more than a philanthropic gesture. The church is more than a social agency; it is more than a political action club organized for the betterment of the human race.

You see, just about any organization or business enterprise can do much of what we do. The telephone company gives dinners to needy families at Thanksgiving. The local fraternity and sorority collect toys for low-income children at Christmas. The government feeds the hungry and gives shelter to the homeless. God is not necessarily on their agenda. In fact, many who have philanthropic tendencies may not even believe in God, though God can use unbelievers to do His work. The church is the only organization and organism that affirms that we do what we do because it is God's will, and because we cannot separate worship from the demands of social justice. It is worship that shapes our spiritual lives, impacting our social agenda.

The questions are: Are we giving our God spiritual junk food, a steady diet of Whoppers and Big Macs? Are we giving God food that fills, but does not nourish; satisfies, but does not sustain; arouses, but does not empower? Is our worship much like George Bernard Shaw's reported commentary on preaching? He says that some preaching is like coffee: it stimulates, but does not nourish. Some is like wine; it has sparkle, but no lasting value. Some is like seltzer water; a big fuss over nothing. And some is like spring water; good, but hard to find. Is our worship like spring water, running deep and quenching our soul's thirst for living water from the living God? Has the church and its worship become too much like the world, with much form, yet without substance? Or even a church of Hollywood glitter where what appears real is nothing more than a set on a Hollywood stage?

While on trip to California some years ago, I visited Universal Studios, where the tour bus passed by a beautiful mansion. The lawn was well manicured. The windows decorated with carved wood. The winding path leading to the front door was inlaid with fine stone. The gate was solid and the spikes from the wrought iron fence pointed toward the California sky. But when we went around in back of the stately mansion, there was nothing. There was no closet in which to hang my coat; no sink in which to wash my hands; no kitchen in which to cook my food; and no bed on which to lay my weary head. It looked like a house, but it was just pretending to be what it was not. From the front, it had height and width; but from the rear, it had no depth. Upon closer examination, not even the front was real. The grass was artificial. The fence, if you leaned on it, would fall. What I thought was wood, was only plastic pretending to be wood. What appeared to be beauty was nothing more than artistic illusion.

Is our worship of God a Hollywood prop? Noise, but no power? Is it just motion, without movement? Quantitative, but not qualitative? And are we like the sons of Aaron offering God *strange fire*?

Before we go any further, let's define worship. Simply put, worship refers to that which is of worth; that which is of value. Worship means *worth*. Christian value is assigning to God, the Creator, ultimate value and worth by God's creatures. Our word *liturgy* comes from a Greek word, which means *the work of the people*. Worship, then, is both worth and work. Both Hebrew and Greek words pointing to Biblical worship give us the idea of bowing down and touching God's hand, as it were, but only because God takes the initiative to be touched, to be known. In other words, God allows us to worship Him. The Bible also speaks of the glory of God, the *Doxa*. Worship is what happens when heaven and earth meet; when human hearts strain and stretch toward communication with the God of creation; when perfect holiness *tabernacles* with imperfect dust. That's Christian worship.

I think the first issue to be raised in the worship of God is to determine whether or not we are involved in worship for the right reasons. William Willimon in his book, *The Bible: A Sustaining Presence in Worship*, rightly suggests that many people are in church, or are in a particular church, because they worship the *cult of me*. The question most raised in our society today is: "What's in it for *me*?" So many people choose churches the way they choose insurance companies: it all depends on whoever gives the best deal and offers the best rate. It's about whoever offers the most in the shortest length of time.

We window-shop for the worship experience that offers the most for the least. We sample worship, but never swallow and digest. It's all about *me*. This church makes *me* feel important; this church recognizes *me* as a person. I can go and drink it all up and, like an over indulgent pet, and leave without giving anything in return. Does this music move *me*? Does the preacher know *my* name? Does the church appreciate *my* gifts?

By the time we are finished in the worship experience, the meaning of "religious experience" has been defined and redefined by *me*. Somehow or another, we see the part, but not the whole. If the Spirit does not touch *me*, it's because the Spirit was not there. If the sermon does not move *me*, it's because the sermon was bad. Although, it might be that you would not know a good sermon if you heard it.

Of course, this is not totally undesirable. The worship service ought to meet our needs. But, the true nature of worship is not *me*-centered, but God-centered. The real question is who's on stage? Who is the main attraction? Who is the subject of every sermon? Who is the audience? Who is the reason around why we gather? Whose name is lifted to the vaulted ceiling, and etched in every stained-glass window?

It is not just a question of whether or not *we* are satisfied, but whether or not God is satisfied. Not only are we God's audience; in worship, God becomes our audience. We never really need to pray for the Holy Spirit to show up. The Lord is already in His house. We do not really have to wait for the Spirit to show up. The Spirit is there waiting for us to show up.

It has to do with our agenda in worship. People come to church with their own agendas. Everybody wants something for himself or herself, looking for something that may or may not have anything to do with God. Some people never hear the song because they are hung up on who's singing the song. They never hear the sermon because they are too busy analyzing the messenger, instead of hearing the message. They sit like amateur psychologists trying to read the preacher's mind, but not hearing the voice of God. So, if the preacher talks too much about trouble, it must be because the preacher is having trouble. If the preacher talks too much about marriage, it must be because the preacher's marriage is on the rocks. Before you know it, we have offered to the Lord *strange fire*.

The next issue I wish to consider is at what point does one become a worshipper? It is possible to come into the sanctuary where worship takes place, go through the order of service, receive the benediction and leave without having worshipped at all. Wearing the garments of worship does not mean that the person wearing the garment is, in fact, worshipping. Putting on an apron does not make one a cook. Wearing a baseball uniform does not make one a baseball player. In fact, it does not necessarily suggest that one roots for the team whose uniform one is wearing. I saw a boy the other day with a Dallas Cowboys' cap, an Atlanta Braves' shirt, and New York Knicks' sweatpants. I asked him what was his favorite team. He answered, "The Indiana Pacers."

The deaconess with the whitest uniform can be the biggest hindrance to ministry. The choir member with the cleanest robe can catch a bad attitude if he or she does not get to sing the solo. The usher with the brightest outfit can have the meanest look on her face. In fact, sometimes the way we dress automatically excludes people in our community who cannot dress like us. Sometimes, the way we worship excludes people in the neighborhood who can find God in the warmth of a storefront, but cannot find Him in our grand cathedrals.

Whatever else worship is, it is an attitude. We cannot change a person's behavior without first changing their attitude. That's why people behave well until they get to where they want to be. However, the attitude often goes unchanged. Remember that Cain's offering was not rejected, nor was Abel's offering accepted merely because God prefers shepherds over farmers. Cain, a farmer, could not worship by giving God his brother's offering.

Perhaps the deeper reason why his offering was rejected had to do with his attitude toward his brother Abel and his disposition toward God. He was already predisposed toward murder. Murder was already in his heart. He just carried out what had already taken up residence in his heart. When our attitude is not one of humility and praise, when we put on the uniform for the wrong reasons, for recognition or for personal glory, we offer, like Nadab and Abihu, *strange fire* unto the Lord, and our spirits die.

Another point that must be made concerning our worship of God is that worship cannot be compartmentalized. Worship in the sanctuary becomes meaningful when the whole of life is seen as an act of worship and praise. The fact is that no man-made sanctuary can confine God. King Solomon was right on target when he raised the question, *Who is able to build Him an house, seeing the heaven of heavens cannot contain Him?* (2 Chronicles 2:6).

God is bigger than the spaces in which we seek to confine Him. God does not belong to any denomination. No creed can contain God. No church can claim exclusive rights to God's unmerited grace. No sect has a monopoly of God's power. No race can ever paint God their color alone! God is bigger than the American flag — a symbol of our country, but not a symbol of our faith — although it hangs in our churches.

Faith and country do not always mix. It is faith that defines country, not country that defines faith.

Life must be seen in its totality as an offering unto God. Jacob, running away from home, found out the night he stopped to rest under the canopy of a star-filled sky, that God can show up anywhere, even in the midst of our loneliness. For God reminds us that even when we are lonely, we are not really alone. When it was all over, Jacob left this lasting testimony, *Surely, the Lord is in this place, and I knew it not. This is none other than the house of the Lord, and this is the gate of heaven* (Gen. 28:16).

Our ancestors saw a relationship between church altar and the family altar. They did not wait until they got to church to feel the warmth of God's presence; they were warm when they arrived. They had already prayed. They kept a song in their hearts and on their lips while they were out in the field plowing. They gathered around the fireplace for Bible reading and devotions. They went to the "meeting", as they called it, with great expectancy. As a result, they were met at the door by the Lord, who said to them, "Come on in, I've been waiting for you."

Another point that must be made is that the Bible is the main source that informs us about worship. We must not be like the church member who said to her pastor, "Reverend, we don't need the Bible; we have Hiscox's manual and the bylaws." Any discussion of worship must be Biblically based. The Bible must be seen as a worship resource, a worship book. Worship is written on every page. The Bible has a great deal to say about the how and why, the meaning, purpose, and importance of worship.

Even on the glorious first day of creation, when the bright light of God's power shattered the primordial darkness, and cosmos replaced chaos, and God called into being worlds that hang on nothing, *God said . . . and it was so*. Look at the record. Genesis 1:6-7; 9; 11; 14-15; 24; 29-30. In between the "*God said* . . . and the *it was so,*" there was no cosmic rebellion, no debate, no committee report, and no discussion. *God said . . . and it was so!* Ever since then, the heavens have declared the glory of God and the firmament has shown forth His handiwork. How could nature not worship God? It was God who called creation into being and set the boundaries for the sun, moon and stars. It was God who made the seasons and then commanded them to rotate in the proper order.

The Bible has worship written on every page. The journey began when, one day, God touched Abraham on the shoulder and sent him forth without chart or compass to a city where God was and is both architect and builder. Wherever the "father of the faithful" journeyed, he always engaged in two activities: he pitched a tent and built an altar. Isaac learned from Abraham, and Jacob from Isaac. They pitched tents and built altars wherever they went. The tent represented their physical need, while the altar represented their spiritual need. It stands to reason that were it not for the God who had said, *I will be with thee*, the people of God would have neither tent to pitch, nor altar to build.

Sad, is it not, that we live in a time when people pitch tents but have stopped building altars? Whenever and wherever one finds a tent with no altar, one will find *strange fire* being offered up to the Lord. Whenever or wherever there is no altar in our lives and along our journeys–no place of worship and praise–God is not taken seriously, and we die.

How many people sit in church every Sunday morning dead? Their worship has become stale and stagnant. They never hear God's voice, never speak God's name. There is no music in their lives, no melodies of the soul, just the dull cadence of a joyless lament cast in a minor key. No feeling that something of great significance is going to happen in worship today. No sense that God is going to do something. No expectation that the Holy Spirit is going to "set our souls on Holy Ghost fire." *Strange fire*.

What a different view we get when we read those majestic pilgrim songs in the collection of Psalms. Psalms 120 through 134 are called, depending on the translation used, *Songs of Degrees, Songs of Ascent* or *Pilgrim Songs*. They were composed and sung by Jewish pilgrims journeying to Jerusalem for the feast days and when the king was enthroned.

Can you hear them singing? They are gathering from all over the land. They are coming from villages and towns. They are marching, coming from the east, west, north, and south. They are traveling, coming from the Plain of Sharon, from Carmel, from Bethel, and from Shiloh. They are on their way from Tekoa and from Ephraim, from Jezereel and the Salt Valley. They have been on the road a long time, but they can almost see the Holy City. It won't be long now. Every step brings them closer to the city of their highest joy.

Can you hear them singing, *I will lift up mine eyes to the hills*? You see, Jerusalem, geographically and theologically, was always up. I will lift *up* mine eyes. I can't see it until I look up. I will never see Jerusalem, or God, looking down. I must lift up mine eyes . . Where does my help come from? *My help comes from the Lord, who made heaven and earth* (Ps. 121:2).

What about all the dangers along the trail? What of the robbers and thieves and cutthroats? What about rest along the journey? What if the lookout fell asleep? Surely, they had to put their trust in Someone other than themselves.

He will not suffer thy foot to be moved. He that keepeth thee will not slumber. He that keepeth Israel shall neither slumber nor sleep (Ps. 121:3).

What about hot days when the sun beats down without mercy, and cool nights with the haunting, howling wind?

The sun shall not smite thee by day, nor the moon by night (Ps. 121:6).

Shall we trust in our bows and arrows, or swords? What about the bars on our windows, the locks on our doors, the police officer patrolling our streets? No!

The Lord shall preserve thy going out and thy coming in (Ps. 121:7).

How long? A day? A month? A year?

From this time forth, and even for evermore (Ps. 121:8).

And they kept on singing:

I was glad when they said unto me, Let us go into the house of the Lord. Our feet shall stand within thy gates, O Jerusalem (Ps. 122:1-2).

And they kept on singing:

If it had not been for the Lord who was on our side . . . (Ps. 124:1).

And they kept on singing:

They that trust in the Lord shall be as Mount Zion, which cannot be removed, but abideth forever (Ps. 125:1).

And they kept on singing:

Except the Lord build the house, they labour in vain that build it; except the Lord keep the city, the watchman waketh but in vain (Ps. 127:1).

And when they reached the gate of the city, they needed somebody to open the gate. So they sang:

Lift up your heads, O ye gates, and be ye lift up ye everlasting doors, and the King of glory shall come in (Ps. 24:7).

Now, the folks inside the gate aren't going to open the gate for just anybody. The gate to the city represented security and safety. It's easy to capture the city once the enemy is inside the gate. We can't let just anybody in the gate.

Who is this king of glory (Ps. 24:8)?

They sang:

The Lord strong and mighty. The Lord mighty in battle. Lift up your heads O ye gates; even lift them up, ye everlasting doors; and the king of glory shall come in (Ps. 24:8-9).

Those inside wanted to be sure, so they ask again,

Who is this king of glory (Ps. 24:10)?

Again, the response is certain:

The Lord of hosts, He is the King of glory (Ps. 24:10).

Strange Fire!

Chapter Two

AND THE HOUSE WAS FILLED WITH SMOKE

In the previous lecture, I attempted to raise a few issues concerning the meaning, function and nature of worship. In worship, the focus is on God, who is our audience and who invites us to come into the divine presence. Worship permeates the whole of life and cannot be compartmentalized. Any discussion of worship must be Biblically based. It is the Bible which serves as our chief worship resource.

In Chapter 5 of 2 Chronicles, there is a description of the building and dedication of the Temple. Of course, God's house had the best of everything. At the dedication, the Jewish historian says that, *The trumpeters and singers were as one, to make one sound to be heard in praising and thanking the Lord* . . . Then they sang this song: *For he is good; for His mercy endureth forever* . . . And that's when it happened . . . *Then the house was filled with smoke.* There was so much smoke until the priests had to step back. *The glory of the Lord had filled the house of God.* So, it seems that here we have the test of real worship. One can know that real worship is taking place by the presence of the smoke. In this chapter, an attempt will be made to focus upon those who are primarily responsible for the smoke. The pastor, or worship leader, the musician and the choir member. Often those who lead in the worship service fail to worship themselves.

I begin with the pastor because the pastor has been given charge of the congregation by virtue of the authority of the pastoral office. Whatever God wanted the Israelites to know or to do as a people was passed on through Moses, their leader. No doubt God speaks to individuals about their own personal lives. But when it came to the vision, the direction, the destiny of the people, God always spoke through God's servant, Moses.

That's where the buck stops. It is the pastor who is ultimately held responsible by the people, and particularly by God, for the welfare of those over whom the pastor has been called to minister. The pastor is the pastor regardless of his or her level of education. The pastor is the pastor whether or not he or she can sing. The pastor is the pastor whether or not he or she is musically trained. The pastor is the pastor of not just a part of the church, but of the whole church, therefore, ultimately in charge of everything pertaining to the church, including the church at worship.

In many instances, however, it is the pastor who is inadvertently part of the problem. At the risk of oversimplification, pastors usually fall into one of two categories. Either the pastor has too little to do with the direction of worship and music in worship, or too much to do with the direction of worship and music in worship. In the former case, the pastor may feel inadequate or insecure in dealing with matters about which he or she knows little. So the pastor takes a *hands off* attitude and winds up only getting involved when there is a fire to put out, which is often too late. By that time, the damage may have been done. In the latter case, the pastor may, also out of feelings of insecurities and inadequacies, move too far in the opposite direction by being too controlling and not allow people to have any freedom and input in the work of ministry.

There are several options for the pastor to consider. If there is a feeling of ignorance or inadequacy in matters pertaining to music and worship, there are worship resources available to inform and prepare the pastor concerning the issues of worship and music ministry. Ministers might take advantage of seminary courses offered dealing with worship and church music (by the way, I am sure that seminaries can do more in the training and development of students in terms of worship in the church). Workshops could be conducted within the contexts of local ministers' conferences, associations and state conventions. The local church might sponsor workshops, seminars and institutes to help pastors, musicians and choir members in their quest to give God more excellent worship. A pastor need not be a musician or singer in order to have some level of training and appreciation for the issues involved in the worship and praise of God. The pastor may not know an eighth note from a half note, a G clef from a bass clef, a sharp from a flat, but he or she ought to seek and recognize authentic worship and music that is pleasing to God. If the pastor wants the smoke to ascend and descend, he or she ought to know where the smoke comes from and how the smoke is made.

The pastor ought to understand what constitutes real worship and know what music is appropriate for what is going on in the worship. The pastor ought to know what is appropriate for a prayer response, an offering response, an introit. If the pastor wants smoke to come, he or she ought to know that we don't sing, *Now the Day is Over*, or, *The Day is Past and Gone*, at the 8:00 a.m. worship service on Sunday morning. The pastor ought to know that the hymn, *When Morning Guilds the Skies,* is not sung during evening worship. The pastor ought to know that songs dealing with the cross have no place in worship on Easter Sunday morning; for the Easter proclamation is not that He died, but that *He lives*. If the pastor wants smoke to come, he or she ought to know that the Christian wedding celebrated in the sanctuary is no place to sing secular love songs. *You Light Up My Life,* does not belong in a sanctuary wedding. Leave *Ribbon in the Sky,* for the reception. The pastor ought to know that the architectural layout of the sanctuary, the position of the pulpit, the placement of the choir and organ, the arrangement of the Communion Table, all may teach and inform the faithful concerning theological belief and practice. The pastor, as resident theologian, must be deliberate and intentional in guiding and directing the worship of God. For worship can never be meaningful to the congregation until it first becomes meaningful to the ones who lead worship.

The order of worship must be carefully planned. It is interesting how much of the order of service deals with God, and how much deals with us. It's hard to focus on God when there is a parade of persons making a thousand announcements about activities, many of which have nothing to do with the mission and message of the church. It's hard for the smoke to descend when politicians with their entourages come to church to make a speech in order to sway voters, but never stay to hear the Gospel. It's hard for the smoke to come when there is no respect for the Lord's house by those who claim to love the Lord. Where is God in all of this? Real worship is not something that just happens by accident. It must be planned by human hands, and then turned over into God's hand so that God's Spirit can breathe upon it. We give order, but the Spirit gives life. We give focus, but the Spirit gives empowerment. We offer the song, but the Spirit makes the song live.

The other category into which many pastors fall is in being too involved in the administration of the ministry of music and worship. It really does not make sense to hire ministers of music or musicians and then do the job for them. If they cannot do the job you want, they should not be there in the first place; and if they are doing the job, let them do it. Give them room to breathe. For by nature, musicians are creative and innovative. Give them the freedom to operate at least within the parameters pastoral expectations.

A minister who sings must be careful not to turn the choir into his or her own personal back-up group by singing all the solos, thereby preempting the choir's function. Music to be sung by the choir should be selected by the musician with input from the pastor. Music to be sung by the congregation, such as the morning hymn, or invitational hymn, should be selected by the pastor. In other words, the pastor must maintain a delicate balance between hands off and hands on; between a policy of *benign neglect* and a policy of over-interference; between doing too little and doing too much; between looking the other way and looking over the shoulder; between no involvement and over-involvement. The key seems to be the minister of music, or musician, or musicians, whatever the case may be. To this role we now turn.

In November 1993, Boyd V. May was laid to rest. For 50 years, he was the Minister of Music in the Mt. Calvary Baptist Church, Newark, New Jersey, my home church, the church where my father has pastored for 48 years. Boyd May attended the Organists and Choir Directors Guild here at the Ministers' Conference for over three decades. His death marked the end of an era in that church, for he represented a breed and generation of organists/musicians rapidly fading from view. He was a consummate church musician. I make a distinction between church musician and a musician who plays for a church, a distinction to which I shall later return.

There were at least three characteristics he possessed that are worthy to be lifted here. First, Boyd May never accepted an engagement for the choir to sing outside the church without clearing it with the pastor. And each Sunday morning before worship, he would check with the pastor for any last-minute instructions or changes. Secondly, in 50 years he was never late. You could count on him sitting on the organ bench at 10:50 a.m. every Sunday morning. In addition, the choir never came to a rehearsal when he was not there, and on time. They never had to wait for him to get there. If anything, he had to wait for them. Thirdly, he insisted that the music in worship be more than one-dimensional. Each worship service usually consisted of anthem, hymn, spiritual and gospel.

I mention this because it highlights the importance of the type of musician needed and the relationship between the musician and the pastor. Let me return again to the distinction between a church musician, and a musician who plays for a church. A church musician not only knows the keys, but also knows the Lord. We cannot assume that because a musician is musically capable that the musician is spiritually grounded. Every pastor understands that there are persons in the church who are willing, but not able, and others who are able, but not willing. Some can, but won't. Some will, but can't.

We all have musicians up in age who have been "at it" for a long time. But, they have just been *hitting at it*. They are sweet and cooperative and will do anything you ask. They are always faithful and supportive. But they just cannot play. They are what I call *hit and miss* musicians. They hit any note and hope it's the right one. They play in *F* while the congregation sings in *G*. And usually the worse they play, the louder they play. We just have to pray for them and turn them over to the Lord.

Then, there are musicians who have ability, but have issues with following and respecting leadership. They are not church-oriented. They can handle keys, but they cannot relate to people. They will go wherever the biggest salary is offered without any sense of loyalty or real commitment to the church of Jesus Christ. For many of them, playing for a church is no more than playing another *gig*; a place to hang their hat until something better comes along.

The church musician, on the other hand, knows the Lord, respects pastoral leadership, even though not always agreeing, and loves the Lord's people. There was a day when the church musicians were themselves products of the church. They came up through the ranks, through Sunday School. He or she played for Church School and, in my own denominational tradition, Baptist Training Union and the Children's Choir. He or she knew church folks and how they behave, because they were also a part of the body. They knew the traditions of the church, appreciated its history, traditions, and spiritual legacy. They knew the great hymns of the church:

'Tis So Sweet to Trust in Jesus; Keep Me Everyday; Jesus is All the World to Me; We May Not Climb the Heavenly Steeps; Hallelujah, 'Tis Done; Father, I Stretch My Hands to Thee; A Mighty Fortress Is Our God; Beams of Heaven,–just to name a few. And because they were real church musicians, smoke was in the house.

There is a new breed on the scene. Many have no connection to — and no appreciation for — our rich music heritage. We are not a one-dimensional people! We have a Marian Anderson and a Mahalia Jackson; a William Warfield and a James Cleveland; a Leontyne Price and the Swan Silvertones. This new breed has no respect for the tradition. And even though I do think there is a difference between tradition and traditionalism, it is the tradition that anchors us. The real test of a musician's metal is how he or she plays *Amazing Grace,* which cannot be hurried. In our tradition, it takes us at least five minutes to get past the word *Amazing*

The Holy Spirit has to *breathe* on the hymn. We need time to fill in the empty spaces with some *soulful glissandos,* some moaning. You can't put a stopwatch to *Amazing Grace.* In or tradition, *Amazing Grace* is not sung as written in the hymnbook. One must apply what black theologians call a *black hermeneutic.*

The new breed has embraced contemporary, *pop* gospel, which has a place if we are to be relevant. Yet, it should not be used at the exclusion of the tradition, and we should not resign ourselves to feed the people what they want at the expense of feeding them what they need. I shall say more about the music offered in worship later.

One of the major problems in the functioning of the minister of music is the danger of elevating oneself to a level equal to or greater than the pastor. The temptation is to use the choir to fulfill the musician's need to be in charge. So, instead of the musician seeing himself or herself as part of the pastor's team, many see themselves as *pastor* of the choir. The choir, then, becomes their little church, where other church members and choir members gravitate and become members of the musician's *congregation*. If the musician has been in a particular church for a long time, he or she has amassed enough power and influence, even though without authority, and if not careful may become a hindrance to the work of the ministry.

The minister of music must be careful not to use the choir to promote his or her own agenda, and like the minister, must not use the choir as his or her back-up group. The choir's purpose is to provide music for the church, not primarily to give concerts in other churches or to put outside engagements ahead of the church's program.

The musician must always keep in mind that the pastor is leader. The pastor may have a third grade education, while the musician may be a graduate of Juilliard, Peabody or the Boston Conservatory. But the pastor is the pastor. It is the pastor's vision that shapes the life of the church. It is the pastor's program that the musician is called upon to support and encourage. It is the pastor's Biblically-based leadership that the musician is expected to support and enhance.

Now, let us finally turn to the choir that has been called, for obvious and not so obvious reasons, the *war department*. Why is this so? What is it about the choir that seems to be a natural breeding ground for strife? Is it because choir members have less religion than other church members? Is it because, by virtue of its function and purpose, the choir attracts a certain kind of person? Is the devil drawn to church music? There always seems to be something going on in the choir. There is always an issue; always a problem; always a crisis. Why is this? Where is the smoke?

Part of the problem may be that we have helped create the monster. We have allowed the choir to occupy a place of exaggerated importance in the church, as if the church cannot get along without it. We have allowed the choir in effect to *kidnap* the church's song and hold the church hostage. In many churches, the choir does all of the singing. Congregational singing is either dead or in intensive care. We have permitted what goes on in the choir stand to become more important than what goes on in the pulpit. We have encouraged the choir to take center stage, and relegated the Word to a sideshow. When the preacher gets up, there is nothing left but a bunch of yawning, fidgety, bored people who use the sermon as a time for sleep or recess, because they need a break after having just finished doing *their thing*. The organist is outside smoking a cigarette, while we hope he or she returns in time for the invitational song.

The real test of whether or not our worship is authentic is the answer to the questions, "What would happen in worship if the choir did not show up?" "Could we still sing unto the Lord or would we be at a complete loss?" "Could we still have church if the organ blew out, if the piano keys were broken?" We have allowed the church to become so specialized and high-tech until we have pushed out the Spirit. We have become too dependent on the choir, allowing it to do all of our singing. Not our ancestors. Many churches of past generations in the south worshipped their God without choir, organ, piano or drums, yet had a song. No trained voices, but a song. We now have music, but we have lost the song.

The problems within the music ministry are magnified and multiplied by the number of choirs. There is a choir for *this* kind of music, a choir for *that* kind of music. There is a choir that sways, a choir that stands still, a choir that sings gospel and a choir that sings anthems. But, underneath, the reasons for the existence of those choirs, is often political. They allow more people to control, more mini-churches to exist, fracturing the body. If you don't believe it, try to merge some of those choirs.

What we often wind up with is pieces of choirs rather than one whole choir; five bad choirs, rather than one good choir, because each choir has developed its own agenda and competes with the other choirs for star billing. Each choir has a Sunday to sing and its own following of church members. The choir members only come to church on their Sunday to sing. They only *shout* off of their singing. They think they own certain songs, and think that if they are color coordinated, if the sway is perfect–and some are swaying west to east, while others are swaying east to west–if they are marching in step, that they are pleasing God when, in fact, they may be pleasing only themselves, and as a result, offering unto the Lord *strange fire*.

You see, we have wrongly identified the problem. When choir members get all bent out of shape deciding the color of their robes, that's not the real problem. The real problem is the decision-making process at work within the choir. The issue is who's making the decisions. The issue is conflict between those who have been in the choir since WW II and the new folks who just got there. This issue is the battle between the young folks and the old folks who, with their mouths, say they want to move over so young folk can take over; but in their hearts don't really mean what they say.

All of this affects worship on Sunday morning because smoke can never fill the house of the Lord with twisted mouths and bad attitudes sitting in the choir stand. When we put our personal agendas ahead of God's agenda, we wind up entertaining ourselves and telling each other, "Child, you all sure did it today. You did your thing." When that happens, God decides to leave and let us do our thing. We cannot assume that just because it's God's house that God's going to stay there while we do our own thing. The reason why the smoke came in the Old Testament text is because they sang as one. There can be more than one choir, yet they can still sing as one. One agenda. One purpose. One focus. One direction. One faith. One Lord. One baptism. They sang as one. Even if there is more than one choir, we ought to at least lift up one song, if we want the smoke to come. Even if the choir members can't read music, we ought to at least lift up one voice, if we want to smoke to come. Even if nothing seems to go right on Sunday morning–the organist is late, the pianist hits the wrong notes, the preacher's sermon is flat, the choir is not on one accord, the ushers are confused, babies are crying, God can get the glory. Worship is not in our hands. Worship is in God's hands; smoke is God's department. If we send the fire up, He will send the smoke down.

Isaiah, how did you know the Lord was in the temple when six-winged seraphim covered their feet and covered their faces as they sang in antiphonal praise, *Holy, holy, holy, is the Lord of host; the whole earth is full of His glory*? Said Isaiah, "I knew the Lord was in the house when the posts of the door moved at the voice of him that cried, and the house was filled with smoke."

What about you, Moses? How did you know that the Lord was up there on Mt. Sinai?

Said Moses, "I knew the Lord was up in the mountain with me when I saw the smoke."

What about it, black slaves? Do you all have anything to say about the smoke on Mt. Sinai?

Yes, we do! *Up on the mountain, where my God spoke; out of His mouth came fire and smoke. Looked all around. It looked so fine. I asked the Lord if all were mine.*

That's what I like about worship. Worship is an alternative to despair. Worship lets us know there is another side. There is something else in this life besides gloom and darkness, sadness and hopelessness, stormy nights and cloudy days. Worship lets me know that life has a *but* side. If life did not have a *but* side, we may as well close the Bible, rope off the pulpit, and put a lock on the front door. Thank God, there is a *but* side.

Listen to our ancestors singing:
Nobody knows the trouble I see, 'but' glory Hallelujah.
Listen to them sing:

I've been buked and I've been scorned, 'but' ain't going to lay my religion down.
Listen to them sing:
I'm troubled in mind, 'but' I'm so glad trouble don't last always.
Listen, they are still singing:
Been in the storm too long, 'but' Hallelujah, the storm is passing over.
Listen:
We preach not ourselves, 'but' Christ Jesus our Lord.
Listen to the apostle Paul:
We are troubled on every side, 'but' not distressed . . .
. . . Perplexed, 'but' not in despair . . .
. . . Persecuted, 'but' not forsaken . . .
. . . Cast down, 'but' not destroyed."
Listen just a little while longer:
While we look not at the things which are seen, 'but' at the things which are not seen; for
the things which are seen are temporal, 'but' the things which are not seen are eternal.
Listen to Jesus:
In the world, ye shall have tribulation, 'but' be of good cheer; I have overcome the world
(John 16:33).
And finally, listen for the music of what we can be:
Beloved, now we are the children of God . . . And it doth not appear what we shall be;
'but' we know that when he shall appear, we shall be like Him, for we shall see Him as He
is.

And the glory of the Lord filled the house of the Lord, and the house was filled with smoke.

CHAPTER THREE
A NEW SONG

In the previous lecture, we examined the roles of those who provide leadership in the worship of God. We discussed the role of pastor as worship leader. The pastor has been given charge of the affairs of the church, including worship, and must assume the role of leadership in the music ministry of the church. He or she must be involved, but not to the point of smothering or stifling the ability of the music ministry to function. We also examined the role of minister of music/musician. He or she is on the pastor's team, and given the charge of participating in the fulfilment of the church's vision. We also looked at some issues concerning the function and purpose of the choir. Some specific problems were examined. The choir does not sing for the church only, but sings with the church. The choir is also congregation. A former professor of mine, Wendell Whalum of Morehouse College, used to say that the choir sings, *to the congregation, for the congregation, and with the congregation.*

In this lecture, I shall attempt to pull some of these insights together and offer what I hope to be practical ways to improve the worship of God, and enhance our desire to offer to the Lord a new song. What can be done to help pastors effectively navigate through, sometimes, treacherous waters? How can the pastor effectively deal with the *war department* and how can we help the war department to *beat their swords into plowshares, and their spears into pruning hooks*? To these issues we now turn.

At the outset of this discussion I must say that every church has its own peculiar personality and make-up. There are forces in the history of every church that help define each church's character and the way the church's members interact. What may work in one church may not work in another. What is good for one church may not be good for another. What can be done immediately in one church, may take several years in another. Every pastor knows, or ought to know, what he or she can do and cannot do.

However, there are general observations, which might be helpful in our quest to give to the Lord our best. One of the key relationships, it seems to me, is the relationship between the pastor and the minister of music. There are three areas of concern.

Let us look, first, at the selection of the minister of music. Who does the selecting? Who conducts the interview? It seems to me that the pastor must have direct input into who is hired to direct the music ministry of the church. This should not be placed in the hands of deacons, trustees, or a music committee. How a musician comes through the door sets the tone for how he or she will operate, and to whom he or she is accountable. The musician is not on the deacons' team or the choir's team. He or she is part of the pastor's team, and must share the pastor's vision. Pastors must be concerned about whether or not they, and the musicians hired, can work together for the purpose of effective ministry. Of course, the pastor should be surrounded with persons who can help evaluate the qualities of prospective candidates. But, ultimately, the pastor should and must make the choice. The minister of music will not be working with deacons or trustees, but directly with the pastor.

The second area of concern is that of accountability. This is very important for the pastor and for the musician because the musician needs to know to whom he or she is accountable. The musician may become frustrated and confused when everybody is giving direction. Musicians should not be forced to take orders from the deacons, trustees, the music committee (if there is one), and the choir. The choir does not hire the musician. The church hires the musician, again, at the direction and through the leadership of the pastor. Therefore, the minister of music's responsibility is not only to the choir. The president or leader of the choir has no authority over the musician. Choir members are not authorized to inform the musician what music to sing, how to sing, or length and content of choir rehearsals.

The third area of concern is that of evaluation. How does one measure the success or failure of the music ministry? If it is good, what makes it good? If it is bad, what makes it bad and how can it be improved? Has the minister of music done a good job? If so, how is it measured? What are the criteria for determining whether or not there is growth? If there is no growth, why not?

There must be regular, intentional, and deliberate communication between the pastor and Minister of Music. Their relationship should be one of mutual respect. No one should be able to go around one to get to the other. In other words, they should watch each other's back. They should be supportive of each other. Nobody should be allowed to go to the pastor and talk about the minister of music; and nobody should be allowed to go to the minister of music and talk about the pastor.

If, in the opening interview with the prospective musician, the first question asked is, "What does the job pay?" that musician may be the wrong person for the job. If, however, he or she asks, "What can I render unto the Lord?" or "How can I use my gifts to enhance the ministry of music in this church under your leadership?" or "What can I do to help bring your vision of God's church into fruition?" then salary negotiation becomes the easy part. Salary compensation ought to be the last hurdle, instead of the first. At that point, the pastor can say, as the vineyard owner said in the parable Jesus told, *Whatsoever is right, I will pay.*

Several factors must be considered in negotiating salary, such as: what are comparable musicians earning in the area? What is the training and experience of the musician? What are the duties and responsibilities, the job description? What are the *real* budget constraints of the church?

There ought to be some realistic goals established; a set of expectations given so that the minister of music's performance can be measured. The goals and expectations ought to be clearly stated from the beginning, and his or her performance evaluated at least once a year, but preferably, several times a year. In this way, a fair assessment can be made as to the musician's leadership skills and ability. It is unfair to tell a person he or she has not done the job, if neither pastor nor musician is clear about responsibilities and expectations.

The second observation is to find ways to reduce an excessive number of choirs in one church to a more effective number. If the number of choirs in a church can be reduced, the number of potential problems also may be reduced as well. It is far better to have one (or two) good adult choir of mixed voices, than to have many fragmented, warring, competitive groups, each doing their own thing. Find ways to bring the choirs together to sing as one, at least on special occasions. These special occasions might be Communion Sundays, revivals, church anniversaries, or sometimes on occasions when the church goes out to fellowship with another church.

There is a risk, of course, and the cost must be counted. Jesus did say that no one should build a tower without first counting the cost to see if there is enough money to build it. If a few choir members, resistant to change, fall by the wayside, it just might become a blessing in disguise. Sometimes quantity must be subtracted, in order for quality to be added. That is the case, so be it. Sometimes we are forced to multiply by subtraction. If a choir member does not have enough *God*

A New Song

within to sing with members of other choirs, he or she may not need to be in the choir in the first place. Maybe he or she is in the way of a new song being sung. New songs cannot be sung with old attitudes in the way, no more than old wineskins are worthy of new wine.

The third observation is that the choir needs to be moved from a *club* mentality to a *ministry* focus. The primary purpose of the choir is spiritual, not social. The focus of the choir must be on worship and music, not fundraising. The choir is not a fundraising group. If it is allowed to degenerate into an organization sponsoring baby contests, fashion shows, and bus trips, all of that business, unrelated to God's kingdom, will seep into the choir rehearsal and into the choir stand on Sunday morning. There is nothing worse than listening to a bunch of angry, discontented choir members trying to sing a joyful song, when they are not joyful themselves. Beautiful robes cannot hide bad attitudes or bad singing.

A fourth observation that should be made is that we, in the church, must seriously begin to *grow* our own musicians. What I mean is that we must provide the context and opportunity for the musical training of our young. If it doesn't happen within the church, it won't happen. If necessary, we need to provide music lessons, both piano and organ, and train our young to be church musicians. Hopefully, they will grow up with love for music and, more important, a love for the Lord. Investing in them now may pay dividends later.

You see, many of us learned about the Lord from the time we first knew our own names. We learned and sang the great hymns and spiritual songs of the church in Sunday School. We were taught the great doctrines of the church in BTU (Baptist Training Union), or some other denominational training ground. We were *church babies*. We lived and breathed church. When we were not in church, we *played* church. We could not wait to partake in our first Communion. We grew up around church folks, within the body of Christ.

When you have been around us long enough, you learn some things about us. We learn not to get offended too easily. We learn that everyone in the church is not perfect, though we serve a perfect God. We learn that we are not in the church because we're good; we are in the church because we are saved. We learn that the quickest way to become discouraged is when one tries to please everybody all the time. We learn that even though one should take God seriously, one must not take one's self too seriously. We learn that the only way to find real peace when we work in the church is to keep remembering for whom we labor. We give God the glory.

A fifth observation is that change involves teaching and training. Not only must we teach the right notes, dynamics and parts–and that should be taught–but also, worship must be taught. Singing a new song goes beyond singing the right notes, knowing the alto part and getting the sway right. There are people who come to church and only meet the Lord by accident. If they see Jesus, it's a surprise. Some, of course, would not even know Jesus if he sat next to them. That is surprising, in light of the fact that when we read the gospels, we discover that even demons knew Jesus' identity. The demons that had control of the man who confronted Jesus in the synagogue in Capernaum, knew Jesus. They were heard saying, *Let us alone; what have we to do with you, Jesus of Nazareth? I know who you are. You are the Holy One of God* (Luke 4:34).

Now, we know that God will show up in unexpected places. Who would have expected God to show up in the middle of nowhere, as Jacob slept under the canopy of a dazzling starlit sky? And when it was all over, the same stone Jacob had used for a pillow became a pillar, bearing witness to the holy presence. And the place where he slept was transformed into the place where he worshipped. Who would have expected God to show up on the dusty plains of a Midian Desert and call a murderer named Moses by name? Who would have expected God to show up in a valley of disconnected, dismembered, disenfranchised, dry, lifeless bones and dare ask the prophet Ezekiel, *Son of man, can these bones live* (Ezek. 37:3)?

Who would have expected God to show up over a sheep pasture on a Judean hillside, and in dazzling splendor announce the birth of His only begotten Son to a bunch of smelly, dirty, unshaven shepherds? Who would have expected God to show up on a desolate isle called Patmos? But God tells John, "John, since you can't come to church, I'll bring church to you." John looked and saw what no humans had ever seen, and heard what no human ears had ever heard. He heard a voice that said, *Behold, I make all things new* (Rev. 21:5). That means: A new city with a new address, a new name, a celestial choir singing a new song.

God can show up anywhere, at any time, anyhow. Yet, God ought to, at least, show up in God's house. Worship just does not happen; worship is planned; and worship is taught. People must be taught how to behave when they are standing on Holy Ground. When we constantly enter worship late and leave early, we dishonor God. When we allow our children to use the hymnals and Bibles as writing pads in order to keep them quiet, we dishonor God. When we turn the offering into recess and walk all over the sanctuary without just cause, we dishonor God. When we turn worship into a circus, and when the church becomes a religious nightclub and a sideshow, we dishonor God. Worship, then, becomes like a sandwich; with one slice of bread called the call to worship, the other slice called the benediction, but no protein in between, just mayonnaise.

Another point to be made is that worship is not a *spectator sport*. It is not for those who wish to remain on the sideline. It is no place for observers. It is no place for people to go and *study* and *examine* worship. Worship is no place for persons to go see how others feel in worship. Worship was and is intended for the worshipper to experience the presence of the

Holy Spirit. Worship is not the place for persons to go to see how the sermon affects others. Persons like that never allow themselves to be confronted by the awesome claims of the Gospel of Jesus Christ. However, when that happens, these same souls, inevitably leave saying, "The preacher sure did tell *them* a thing or two."

For a life-transforming experience of worship to take place, there must be an intentional emphasis on congregational singing. The great hymns, which have nurtured and fed our faith, need to be lifted. After all, it is our hymns that contain our rich theology. Our hymns remind us who God is, and what God is like. Our hymns speak of God's glory and majesty, power and might. Our hymns are cast in great poetic cadences and contain imagery that stretches the imagination. Our hymns give us spiritual snapshots of a land fairer than day. Our hymns take us from that far away garden where Adam sinned all the way to that celestial city where Jesus will reign forever and ever. What "poetic imagination," which lifts our souls to realms of day beyond the earthly dust; up where the spirit soars on the wings of eagles.

> *Must I be carried to the skies*
> *On flowery beds of ease,*
> *While others fought to win the prize,*
> *And sailed through bloody seas?*

What about those Spirituals? What about those majestic songs that tell of our particular pilgrimage as a people in pain, sons and daughters of African soil, pulled from the motherland and left to rot in a pigpen called slavery? What about them? Yet, somebody out in a cotton field started "moaning," others joined in, and in spite of the stench of slavery, they looked up and started singing, *Over my head, I hear music in the air. There must be a God somewhere.*

Those Spirituals were passed down from generation to generation. A self-made preacher in South Philadelphia, Charles Albert Tindley, caught fire and started singing:

> *If the world from you withhold*
> *All its silver and its gold,*
> *And you try to get along with meager fare.*
> *Just remember in His word*
> *How he feeds the little bird.*
> *Take your burden to the Lord and leave it there.*

It was the son of a country preacher down in Georgia, by the name of Thomas Dorsey, who caught fire and started singing, *Precious Lord, take my hand* . . .

In the windy city known as Chicago, a girl with a golden voice, whose name was Mahalia Jackson, caught fire and started singing, *Move on Up a Little Higher*.

In South Philadelphia, on Fitzwater Street, in the Union Baptist Church, a girl named Marian Anderson opened her mouth and music came out. One day she stood on the steps of the Lincoln Memorial and sang, *He's Got the Whole World in His Hands*.

And back in the windy city, Roberta Martin Singers started singing, *Only a Look*.

The man who wrote songs for Roberta Martin–James Cleveland–caught fire and started singing, *Peace, Be Still*. The fire spread to the west coast, where Edwin Hawkins started singing, *O, Happy Day*.

In addition, worship is about remembering. There are some people who have suggested that we ought to forget. They say our past is an embarrassment, a hindrance to our progress. We ought to forget that we were once in Egypt. Some suggest that we Forget our Spirituals, the split verbs, the *dis heres* and *dat dares*, the *Git on Board, Lil' Chillen*, remnants and reminders of a slave past. The say we ought to shed our slave names, the names given to us when first we saw the light of day.

Don't they know that changing names does not ensure a change in character? Don't they know that if you are a liar with an old name, and change names, you are still a liar with a new name? Don't they know that names are changed, not from below, but from above? That's why our ancestors sang, *I know I've been changed, the angels in the heaven done signed my name.* But, you know these are the same folks who, back in the sixties and seventies, predicted the demise of the black church, because in their minds the black church was no longer relevant.

Rather than forgetting, as these people suggest, it seems that we ought to remember.

How have the people of Jewish ancestry been able to keep on clawing through history, against the odds? They did what the Lord told them to do. They gathered throughout the year to remember what the Lord had done.

Remember how the Lord brought you out of Egypt.

Remember how the Lord opened up the Red Sea, and you did not even get your sandals wet.

Remember how the Lord guided you through the wilderness with a pillar of cloud, by day, and a pillar of fire by night.

Remember how, when the trumpets blew, the walls of Jericho came tumbling down.

Remember how the Lord gave you victories over the Amorites, Perrizites, Jebusites, and Hittites.

Remember how the Lord gave you a land called Canaan, flowing with milk and honey.

Don't forget. Remember.

Remember now thy Creator in the days of thy youth . . . (Ecclesiastes 12:1).

If I forget thee, O Jerusalem, let my right hand forget her cunning (Psalms 137:5).

Worship is a remembering; a dramatic reenactment of God's mighty acts. When black folks get together on the Lord's Day, we have something to remember.

Remember that we, too, were slaves in an Egypt, called America.

Remember segregated lunch counters and Jim Crow laws and making brick without straw.

Remember hard times and lonely nights and dark days.

Remember those old illiterate country preachers, who told us a better day is coming.

Remember how the Lord has brought us a mighty long way.

Remember the songs grandmother used to sing. And even though she may be resting in her grave, the song still lives.

Remember those saints who would shout if you just called the name, Jesus.

Remember.

Remember that what the Lord will do is predicated on what the Lord has already done.

When David, the scrawny, frail shepherd boy, went out to meet the giant named Goliath, Saul wanted to know, "What makes you think you can whip Goliath?"

David responded, "Mr. King Saul, one day I was tending the sheep of my father Jesse, and a lion snatched one of the sheep; I killed the lion and rescued the sheep. Not only that, but on another occasion, a bear sneaked in and plucked up one of the lambs; I killed the bear and rescued the lamb. And based on my remembrance of what the Lord has already done, I am sure that he will be with me when I go out to meet Goliath."

I do not need to tell you what happened. When the dust had cleared, David was marching in a ticker-tape parade down Main Street, and women were dancing and singing this song:

Strange Fire

Saul has killed his thousands, but David, his ten thousands (1 Samuel 29:5).

Worship takes place in the remembering of the promises of God.

I don't know about you, but when I walk out on the pulpit on Sunday morning, I do not necessarily want to hear Bach's *Fifth Symphony in G Minor*, because I am looking out into the face of a mother who just buried her son who died from an overdose of cocaine. She raised him in Sunday School, faithfully brought him to church every Sunday morning. She does not need to hear Bach, Beethoven, or Brahms. However, a song *is* in order. She needs to hear the organ play; *He knows just how much you can bear.*

I'm looking out into the face of a young man who just finished college. He graduated in the top of his class and is getting ready to enter a master's program. But he just found out that he has terminal cancer. Well, a song *is* in order. He needs to hear, *Father, I stretch my hand to thee. No other help I know. If thou withdraw thyself from me, ah, whither shall I go?*

I see over in the choir stand a woman who just learned that her husband doesn't love her anymore because she's getting old and unattractive. Well, a song *is* in order. *When I'm growing old and feeble, stand by me. When my life becomes a burden, and I'm nearing chilly Jordan, oh thou Lily of the Valley, stand by me.*

I see a young person over to my left who had no choice but to put her mother in a nursing home; and she now feels guilty and ashamed. I think a song *is* in order.

Look who just walked in. A young man who has contracted the AIDS virus. Church people, who once were loving and kind, have now turned mean and nasty and whisper behind his back. They are telling him that God does not love him anymore. Well, a song *is* in order. A simple song that you learned on your mother's knee, *Jesus loves me, this I know, for the Bible tells me so.*

There is an old saint walking to her seat with a walking cane, and it's taking her a little while to get there. It seems as though a parishioner does not want to be bothered getting up to let her in the pew. At home, her daughter does not care about her anymore, even though this old lady scrubbed floors to send her to college. I think she needs to hear a song. What shall it be? *Be not dismayed whate'er be-tide, God will take care of you; Beneath His wings of love abide, God will take care of you.*

There is an old faithful deacon sitting on the front pew. His mother is gone; his father is gone; all of his sisters are gone; his brothers are gone. He has no children to comfort him. His friends are gone. He feels lonely and all by himself. He needs a song: *I've seen the lightning flashing; I've heard the thunder roar . . . No, never alone. No, never alone. He promised never to leave me, never to leave me alone.*

CHAPTER FOUR

AN UNCERTAIN SOUND

During these next three lectures, I will seek to focus again on issues concerning our worship of God. In this lecture, I wish to identify and give commentary to some dangerous trends taking place in the church, thereby affecting our worship of God. Keep in mind that worship refers to *that which is of worth* or something of value. Christian worship, then, is assigning ultimate value and worth to God, who is Creator, Sustainer, and Redeemer. Worship is our total human response to all that God has done and all God is. In the next lecture, I will attempt to look more closely at the order of service, making some general and specific comments on how we can enhance our understanding of what we do in worship. In the third and final lecture, I will seek to focus on the Christian funeral, and place it, along with the matters of death and dying, within the context of worship.

As we approach the dawning of the 21st century and look out over the landscape of our religious faith and practice, it seems clear that there are several trends which affect the way we view God, thereby affecting the way we worship God. Like it or not, the church is, at least, *in* the world, if not *of* the world. The question to be considered in this fourth lecture is this: To what extent does what happens *outside* the sanctuary, affect what happens *inside* the sanctuary? A companion question is: To what extent does what happens inside the sanctuary affect what happens in the world? I have labeled this lecture, *An Uncertain Sound*.

The people of God do not worship in a vacuum or in some incubator, separated and protected from the world. Even though we worship in the sanctuary, we work in the world, we witness in the world, and we live in the world. The church building itself does not occupy space in some celestial realm, where streets are paved with gold, and where saints chant perpetual *Hallelujahs*, and where church doors are left unlocked because there is no crime. In fact, in *that* celestial city, there is no temple. Our churches do not reside in some magical wonderland beyond the skies, although there was a day when churches and homes were left unlocked.

However, for the most part we do take up residence in mean cities, on mean streets, in dingy, dark alleys, surrounded by the stench of garbage, the noise of boom boxes keeping their steady beat of profane lyrics, the sounds of mothers high on crack cursing their babies, the shrill noises of honking horns, police sirens, the wheels of fire trucks rolling, and the slam of a basketball hitting the playground pavement. We may sing, *Holy, Holy, Holy*, but even as we sing we are surrounded by the unholy, the irreligious, the sacrilegious, the ungodly, the indecent and the irreverent. Yes, like it or not, we are a part of the very world we seek to win for Christ. We live and move, worship and work, to borrow the title of a book by John Stott, *Between Two Worlds*.

The church always operates somewhere between this world and the world to come. If we drift too far into the world of the hereafter, we run the risk of becoming an irrelevant and useless voice of personal piety, just sitting back waiting for the rapture, unconcerned about the real world, a world where people are hurting and in pain, a kind of, *I've got mine, and that's enough* religion.

If the church tilts too far into the affairs of this present age, it reduces itself to a philanthropic society, a social agency, a self-help center void of any spiritual content and focus, thereby ceasing to be the church of Jesus Christ. For Jesus was more than a social reformer, and we should all know by now that people can enjoy productive employment, decent housing in which to live, adequate medical care, food on the table, clothes in the closet, a television and video cassette recorder in every room, and still be lost.

Even though these bread and butter issues ought to be a part of the church's agenda, the church must always point people to something higher than economic, social and political well-being. When the disciples came up to Jesus admonishing Him to eat because He was hungry, His response was, *I have food to eat of which you do not know* (John 4:32).

Each Sunday morning, the saints gather in the sanctuary of the Lord, seeking this bread. They may come late, and leave early. They may not seem to take worship seriously. They may come with their own agendas. They may appear disinterested and unconcerned. They may not even understand fully why they are there, yet Sunday after Sunday they show up. And in the deep places of their hearts, where only God is qualified to search, their need is the same as the need expressed by a nameless woman of Samaria, who stood before the Master at Jacob's well. And what started out with Jesus asking her for a drink, ended up with her asking Him for a drink of living water, *Sir, give me this water, so that I may never be thirsty or have to keep coming here to draw water* (John 4:15).

When we turn to the New Testament record, we do not get a portrait of a worshipping community being led by the culture, but rather of a worshipping community, whose worship was so empowering that the culture was never the same. Each time the new converts began to yield to practices and traditions contrary to the ways and will of God, the apostles kept reminding them of who they were, who they were called to be, and whom they represented. *But you are a chosen generation, a royal priesthood, a holy nation, a peculiar people; that you should show forth the praises of Him who has called you out of darkness into His marvelous light* (1 Peter 2:9). *So if anyone is in Christ, there is a new creation: everything old has passed away; see, everything has become new* (1 Cor. 5:17) When Luke summarizes the impact of Philip's preaching in Samaria, he says, *And there was great joy in that city* (Acts 8:8). Why? Because the worship of God is dynamic, inspiring, and transforming. We must not allow the world to define who we are as a worshipping community. We must not be intimidated by the glitzy churches, with their *Hollywood* approach to the gospel, or try to package, sell, and market the Gospel, as if it is a bottle of Coca-Cola.

I contend that the possibilities for empowerment and transformation are evident within the context of worship. The New Testament church was Spirit-filled, not just a noise-filled assembly. For there are noises and there are *holy noises*. The New Testament church transformed the lives of people and gave them newness of life. The blind received their sight, the lame walked, the lepers were cleansed of their ugly spots, the dead were raised, the ears of the deaf were opened, the poor heard the good news of the Gospel preached by fearless apostles. The Kingdom of God *is* breaking in. God had visited the earth in the person of God's Son, Jesus, and men and women, with whom He walked and talked, saw in His eyes the spark of divinity and on His forehead the stamp of His Father's approval. Their testimony was this, *We have seen the Lord!* There was something about the *why* and the *how* of worship that had the power to transform weak, frightened disciples into bold and courageous proclaimers of the good news.

We must remember that in the early church, each Lord's Day was a celebration of the Resurrection. Resurrection was not celebrated once a year, but every Sunday on the first day of the week. The central truth of the Resurrection brought despondent disciples back from their fishing boats by the Sea of Galilee to an upper room where Peter, who had denied his Lord, now begins to proclaim Him boldly. The central claim of the Resurrection changed the day of worship from the last day of the week to the first day of the week.

Wouldn't our worship be more powerful and transforming if we gathered each Sunday to celebrate Resurrection, minus the Easter trappings? Not Easter bunnies, eggs, parades and new clothes; but this: *If Christ be not risen, your faith is in vain and you are yet in your sins* (1 Cor. 15:17). If we knew the impact of the Resurrection, even Easter Sunday could be transformed into Resurrection Sunday. The worst thing we can do to chill and dampen the Resurrection story on Easter Sunday is to sing songs with the focus on Calvary and the cross. Resurrection Sunday is no time to sing, *Jesus, Keep Me Near the Cross*. On Easter Sunday, *At the Cross,* must give way to, *Christ the Lord is Risen Today, Alleluia!* Much of our Sunday morning worship sounds more like a funeral dirge than an *ode to joy*.

As stated in the outset, the title of this lecture is, *An Uncertain Sound*. Paul, the apostle to the Gentiles, has a great deal to say about worship. In the letter we call I Corinthians, the great apostle to the Gentiles addresses matters regarding appropriate and authentic worship. It is impossible to understand the 13th chapter without reading and understanding the 12th chapter, which is about spiritual gifts. He closes the 12th chapter by saying, *But strive for the greater gifts, and I will show you a more excellent way*. The more excellent way is described in the 13th chapter, which begins, *If I speak with the tongues of men and of angels, but do not have love, I am a noisy gong or a clanging cymbal*. Then, chapter 14 is an extension of what has been laid out in chapter 13. For he begins chapter 14 with this admonition, *Pursue love and strive for spiritual gifts . . .*

Paul goes on to talk about the confusion that arises in our worship of God when there is no clear focus, no purpose, no order, no sense of direction, when we get caught up in doing our own thing and trying to put forth our own petty agendas that have nothing to do with the Lord. Paul puts it this way, *If the trumpet give an uncertain sound, who will get ready for the battle* (1 Cor. 4:8)? Today, there are some uncertain sounds, several trends, which pose a threat to the empowerment that can come through authentic Spirit-filled worship.

The first I call the pre-empting of the cross. It is an easily recognizable symbol, known universally by Christians and non-Christians alike. The cross is stamped on our church steeples, our sanctuary lighting, our pews, our robes, our church doors, our offering plates, our Bibles and hymnals. Crosses hang on chains over our pulpits. Some are made of gold or some other precious metal. They come in all sizes and designs. They are worn as ornaments. Professing Christ as one's savior is not a prerequisite for purchasing one from the local jeweler. One need not offer a confession of faith before placing a cross around the neck or ankle. It looks pretty; it's stylish. For many, it's a fashion statement and that's all. But that's the point. When it comes to the cross of Christ we have cleaned, dressed it up in unfamiliar garments. The message of the cross is muted, thereby rendering it *an uncertain sound*.

We have taken this symbol of suffering and shame, this representation of unyielding love and redemptive power, and made it respectable. We have moved the cross from a garbage heap outside Jerusalem and relocated it to more respectable living quarters. We have wiped away the blood from the tree and we have muted the groans of the One who hung there crying, *My God, My God, why hast thou forsaken me* (Mat. 27:46)? There is no longer any trace of the suffering, the agony, the death rattle, the last sigh, the final breath or the limp and lifeless body of the lowly carpenter from Nazareth.

As a result, suffering has become a bad word. We are now told by the *name-it-and-claim-it* crowd, that whatever we want is at our fingertips, if we want it bad enough. We do not have to suffer, just ask. It's not a matter of whether or not it's in God's will. Just ask. There is more emphasis on our works than on God's grace. We have turned religion into a blessing factory. We want blessings, without burdens. We want results, without responsibility. We want power, without struggle. We want the God who provides, but not the God who tests. We want the victory, without the wrestling with God until the dawning of the day. Remember, Jacob left the divine presence with his blessing, but also with a limp.

We have misinterpreted the words of Jesus, who said to the disciples, *Ask what you will, and it shall be given unto you* (John 15:7). We want the *ask* without the *if*, forgetting that the *ask* is predicated on a divine *if*. Not simply, *ask what you will* . . . but rather, *If you abide in me, and my words abide in you, [then] ask* . . .

Now, the last thing we want to do is to deify suffering. Bragging about suffering is just as bad as complaining about it. Some people are too proud of their battle scars, especially those self-inflicted scars, resulting from the sins of arrogance and pride. Some people use their suffering as an excuse to do nothing, as if God ordained that they would go through life having a hard time. So, they want to celebrate their hard times through song and testimony.

> *I'm climbing up the rough side of the mountain . . .*
> *I'm doing my best to make it in.*
> *I'm trampin', trampin', trying to make heaven*
> *my home.*
> *See me toiling, trying to make a hundred; ninety-nine*
> *and a half won't do . . .*

By redemptive suffering we are talking about the struggle that comes from hearing and doing the will of God. It is not our personal crosses we are compelled to bear, but the cross of Christ.

In much of our modern worship this idea of struggle seems absent, even in songs that help shape our theology as well as the theology that helps give shape to our songs. Our songs reflect who we are as a worshipping community. Our songs have been pre-empted by the world, thereby neutralized. Many gospel singers and musicians have fought a long and hard battle to gain respectability and recognition on the world's entertainment stage. Now, we have been given our just due at the Grammy's. Finally, our music has been recognized. There are even several categories of gospel music. There is a rock gospel category, a pop contemporary category, a southern bluegrass category, a traditional soul gospel category, a contemporary gospel category, and more in the future.

Now, *When the Saints Go Marching In,* is being sung on stage, and by college and high school marching bands during halftime performances at nationally televised football games. Now, *Amazing Grace,* has become a favorite on television variety shows. Our music has made the "big-time," crossing over from sanctuary to stage.

This is good, I suppose. Certainly the desire to gain universal acceptance is well intended. Yet, it comes with a price. The price is that we have wiped away Jesus' blood for the sake of acceptability, respectability, and popularity. We have allowed *Amazing Grace* to be neutralized because it no longer offends anybody. It has been taken out of its context, snatched from the soil where its roots run deep, relocated from the sanctuary and sacred places, where its eternal message was clear and transforming, and placed on a glittering stage behind roving cameras, where it has been given another meaning and message.

We have taken the choir robe off of *Amazing Grace* and put on her a silky evening gown of respectability. Now Tony Bennett, Frank Sinatra, Stevie Wonder, Michael Jackson, and Luther Vandross join hands on stage, black and white together, Jew and Gentile, Muslim and Christian, right wing Republicans and liberal Democrats, and sing, *Through many dangers toils and snares . . .* One can sing religious lyrics without assigning to those lyrics religious content, an *uncertain sound*. When sung out of context, the world pre-empties our sacred songs of any religious content. In order to sign contracts, some religious singers agree not to use the name *Jesus*.

Yet, how can one avoid His name? Why, He is His name. *Thou shalt call His name Jesus, for He shall save His people from their sins* (Mat.1:21) . . . *If ye ask anything in my name, I will do it* (John 14:14) . . . *In the name of Jesus Christ of Nazareth, rise up and walk* (Acts 3:6). Not call His name? *Whosoever shall call upon the name of the Lord shall be saved* (Rom. 10:13) . . . *For there is none other name under heaven given among men, whereby we must be saved* (Acts 4:12)

Not call His name?

Wherefore God also hath highly exalted Him, and given Him a name that is above every name; that at the name of Jesus, every knee shall bow; of things in heaven, and things in earth, and things under the earth; and that every tongue should confess that Jesus Christ is Lord, to the glory of God the Father (Phil. 2:9-10) . . . *How sweet the name of Jesus sounds, in a believer's ear; it soothes the sorrows, heals the wounds, and drives away all fear.* Not call His name? *Jesus, let all saints proclaim, His worthy praise forever.*

When the saints sing, *Amazing Grace*, we know what we are singing about. We know of whom we sing. Grace is not the name of a high school sweetheart. Grace is not some neutral, non-emotional, philosophical, abstract concept. Grace is not a sentimental, mushy, soupy, syrupy idea. Grace is God's unmerited favor. It's about God loving the unlovable; forgiving the unforgivable; accepting the unacceptable; touching the untouchable. It's a son coming back home from a pigpen, and a man from Tarsus preaching with a thorn in his flesh. When we lift our music from the soil of worship and place it on the entertainment stage, we run the risk of hearing an uncertain sound. *If the trumpet give an uncertain sound, who shall prepare for the battle?*

Another dangerous trend in our worship of God is the advent of so-called praise music. Praise music is not a problem in and of itself, as long as we understand what we mean by *praise music*. It is the misapplication of the term that is of concern. There is nothing wrong with praise teams and moments of praise before worship, which in many churches have replaced the traditional devotional period, which Harold Dean Trulear calls *the black church's introit*.

However, what is disturbing is the divorcing of praise from worship, as if they are two completely different activities of the worshipping community. We must remember that praise, even though used as a prelude to worship, is also woven into the very fabric of worship. Worship is more than praise. Our praise songs must reflect a deeper theological understanding of the nature of God and our response to God's love.

Herein lies the abiding value of the Negro Spiritual. The Negro Spiritual always kept in view the creative tension between the goodness of God and the harsh and inhuman realities of the present world. The slave's night was always kept in tension with God's new morning. There was a balance between frustration and hope; between sorrow and joy; between doubt and faith; between dreams deferred and hope realized; between prayer and promise; between today and tomorrow; between death and life; between Satan and God; between the gloom of Good Friday and the glory of the Resurrection morn.

Praise music is attractive because it does not demand much. It does not cost much. It does not require much. It does not contain much theology. It inspires, but does not inform. There is no struggle, no agonizing, no pathos, and no tension, just praise. And if we are not careful, we will render *an uncertain* sound. Praise is good, as long as we balance our praise music with hymns and spiritual songs that tell us who God is, what God requires, who we are and how we must respond to God's love. Now, all of our hymns do not contain good theology, to be sure. But, at least they do contain theology, and therefore, call us to theological reflection.

This brings me to another disturbing trend. We should all be disturbed by some attempts to completely throw out our tradition, and replace it with a *new and improved* version. In an attempt to fashion a new church with a new worship agenda, including all new songs, the architects of these contemporary movements seem to have no appreciation or respect for what brought us. They want to dismantle the tradition, rather than build onto the tradition. They want to subtract, rather than add. They want to act as if we had nothing until they came along. Strange voices are telling us that the old way is the wrong way. They are saying that if we want the presence of the Holy Spirit, as they define it, that we must embrace *this*, *that*, and *the other*, in other words, worship *their* way. We must be all things to all people, so they say. We must throw away the hymnals because they are dated. We become relevant by being theologically shallow. If we are not careful, the trumpet will give forth *an uncertain sound*.

When we look at the Old Testament witness, we get a different view. I see Isaac digging *again* the wells of his father, Abraham. Isaac's digging of old wells represented continuity with past and future. He was a vital link between his father, who went searching for a city, and his son, who was given a new name, as he wrestled with the divine presence. Isaac was a bridge between the faith of his father and the promise of generations unborn. He was a vital connection between yesterday and tomorrow, and also, between the have *been* and the *will be*. Isaac proved that there is yet some good water, clear refreshing, nourishing water in old wells. But they must be dug again.

Can you imagine Jews of the Old Testament telling their sons and daughters to trash the tradition of the fathers and mothers of their ancient but living faith? *Hear, O Israel: The Lord, our God is one Lord . . . These words which I command you this day shall be in thine heart . . . Thou shalt teach them diligently unto thy children, and shalt talk of them thou sitteth in thine house, and when thou walkest by the way, and when thou liest down, and when thou riseth up . . . And thou shalt bind them for a sign upon thine hand, and they shall be as frontlets between thine eyes . . . And thou shalt write them upon the posts of thy house, and on thy gates . . . Then beware lest thou forget the Lord who brought thee forth out of the land of Egypt, from the house of bondage* (Deut. 6:4-9, 12).

Another disturbing trend is the movement toward polite applause in worship, particularly programmed applause. I have a problem with telling people when to start applauding and when to stop, as if the Spirit can be controlled and condensed into a 30-second sound bite. That's an *uncertain sound*. While clapping is an authentic and desirable response in worship, applause that mimics the world is an unwanted intrusion into the sanctuary, which is God's peculiar and particular space. Now, to be sure, the clapping of hands has Biblical significance, particularly when we look at worship in the Old Testament. The psalmist says, *Clap your hands, all ye people; shout unto God with the voice of triumph* (Ps. 47:1).

Even nature joins in. Isaiah prophecies, *For you shall go out in joy, and be led back in peace; the mountains and the hills before you shall burst into song, and all the trees of the field shall clap their hands* (Isaiah 55:12). Hands were made to clap. But clapping, as any other response in worship, is like the wind. It cannot be programmed. One cannot be told when to start clapping and when to stop clapping. Can any of us control the wind? Other than the Master of earth and sea, can we command the wind to stop blowing? Will the wind listen to any other voice but the voice that gave the wind her strength?

The wind blows where it chooses . . . said Jesus to a nighttime visitor named Nicodemus. *You hear the sound of it, but you do not know where it comes from or where it goes* (John 3:8). If we are not careful with our applause, we won't know where we are; we won't know whether it's Sunday morning or Saturday night.

When reading the Bible, it is clear that *Amen* is and always will be an appropriate response in the worship of God. You know you are in church when you can hear somebody say, *Amen*. It is the sweet melody of the whole Bible, written on just about every page. There is nothing quite like hearing the saints say, *Amen*.

When we hear *Amen*, we know where we are. We know what day of the week it is. If we cannot say anything else, we ought to at least say, *Amen*. That's the Biblical response to the truth of the Gospel.

Amen is God's punctuation mark.

Amen is the sweet melody of the soul.

When the priest in the temple gave the benediction and said, "Blessed be the Lord," and the congregation replied, "Amen."

Amen means, "it is so!"

Amen means, "verily, verily . . . truly, truly."

Amen means, "surely, surely."

It means to be firm, true, and reliable.

Jesus Christ is the great *Amen*.

There is an *Amen* at the end of the book of Romans. *To the only wise God, be glory through Jesus Christ forever, Amen.*

There is an *Amen* at the end of I Corinthians. *My love be with you all in Christ Jesus, Amen.*

There is an *Amen* at the end of II Corinthians. *The grace of the Lord Jesus Christ, and the love of God, and the communion of the Holy Ghost be with you all, Amen.*

In Galatians, *Amen* rings out: *. . . the grace of our Lord Jesus Christ be with your spirit, Amen.*

Ephesians proclaims it: *Grace be with all them that love our Lord Jesus Christ in sincerity, Amen.*

Philippians shouts it: *The grace of our Lord Jesus Christ be with you all, Amen.*

Thessalonians extols it: *The grace of our Lord Jesus Christ be with you, Amen.*

Jude heralds it: *To the only wise God our Savior, be glory and majesty, dominion and power, both now and forever, Amen.*

And don't turn to Revelation. *[He] hath made us kings and priests unto God and his Father; to Him be glory and dominion for ever and ever, Amen* (1:6).

Be*hold, he cometh with cloud; and every eye shall see Him, and they also which pierced Him: and all kindreds of the earth shall wail because of Him. Even so, Amen.* (1:7)

And all the angels stood round about the throne, and about the elders and the four beasts, and fell before the throne on their faces, and worshipped God, saying, Amen: Blessing, and glory, and wisdom, and thanksgiving, and honour, and power, and might, be unto our God for ever and ever, Amen (7:11-12).

And the four and twenty elders and the four beasts fell down and worshipped God that sat on the throne, saying, Amen . . . (19:4)

He which testifieth these things saith, Surely I come quickly. Amen. Even so, come, Lord Jesus. The grace of our Lord Jesus Christ be with you all. Amen (22:20-21).

For if the trumpet give an uncertain sound, who shall prepare for battle?

The sound of the trumpet means that something important is about to take place. The trumpet sounding at the foot of Mt. Sinai was the signal for Moses to meet God at the top of the mountain. God tells Moses to make two silver trumpets and let the sons of Aaron blow them to assemble the congregation together.

The Lord says to Joshua after the sons and daughters of Jacob had crossed the Jordan into Canaan, *Let seven priests march around Jericho for seven days, and on the seventh day, the priests shall blow the trumpets, and the walls of Jericho will come tumbling down (Joshua 6:20).*

When Solomon had finished the temple, they brought the Ark of the Covenant, and while the Levites, arrayed in white linen, played their cymbals and psalteries and harps, 120 priests sounded the trumpets.

The Lord says to Isaiah, *Lift up thy voice like a trumpet, and show my people their transgression, and the house of Jacob their sins* (Isaiah 58:1).

The Lord says to Ezekiel, *Then whosoever heareth the sound of the trumpet, and taketh not warning; if the sword come, and take him away, his blood shall be upon his own head* (Ez. 33:4).

The psalmist says, Praise Him with the sound of the trumpet (Ps. 150:3).

The trumpet is God's instrument for battle. When the army is ready for battle, a violin won't do. A harp isn't good enough. Not for the battle. The battle is serious business. We need somebody to blow the trumpet, not with an uncertain sound, but with a distinct sound. If the sound is uncertain, the troops won't know whether to go forward or backward, to charge or retreat. You do not want the army charging, when it ought to be retreating, or retreating when it ought to be charging.

When the end shall come, when time shall shake hands with eternity, when the final *Amen* has been sounded . . .

When the last chapter has ended, and the final song has been sung . . .

When all for which we have waited has finally come to pass . . .

Strange Fire

When the saints go marching in . . . in that great gittin' up mornin' . . .

When Gabriel, who has been practicing since the dawn of creation, shall wing his way toward earth and stand on the highest mountain, he had better hit the right note. His trumpet had better give the right sound; for that will be the signal for the dead in Christ to rise. Not just any dead; but the dead in Christ . . . the dead who have been redeemed . . . the dead whose garments have been washed in the blood of the lamb.

Get it right, Gabriel! Hit the right note.

If you hit the wrong note, the wrong folks will rise.

If you hit the wrong note, atheists will rise.

If you hit the wrong note, cutthroats will rise.

If you hit the wrong note, drug pushers will rise.

If you hit the wrong note, unbelievers will rise.

If you hit the wrong note, Pharaoh, Ahab, and Jezebel, will rise.

If you hit the wrong note, Nero, Mussolini, and Hitler will rise.

If you hit the wrong note, Lee Harvey Oswald, Byron De La Beckwith, Bull Connor, and James Earl Ray will rise.

Hit the right note, Gabriel!

You have been practicing long enough. You have been in rehearsal since the morning stars sang together.

Hit the right note, Gabriel!

Behold, I show you a mystery; We shall not all sleep, but we shall be changed in the twinkling of an eye, at the last trump; for the trumpet shall sound, and the dead in Christ shall be raised incorruptible, and we shall be changed (1 Cor. 15:52).

Hit the right note, Gabriel!

Chapter Five
THE ROMANCE OF WORSHIP

In the previous lecture, we tried to identify some trends that can either enhance or detract from the authentic worship of God. Now we turn to the worship service itself. In 1971, rhythm and blues singer and Motown recording artist, the late Marvin Gaye, popularized a song. In the song, he raised the question, *What's going on?*

I think that's a good question to ask whenever we walk into the sanctuary. *What's going on?* Which leads us to other questions: What are we really doing here? What are we going to do when we leave here? What are we going to do in here that we cannot do somewhere else? Why not stay home? Or the deeper question: Is the Lord in this place?

"Of course the Lord is in this place," you reply. It's God's house. It is the place where God promised to dwell. God's signature is all over the place, written on every pew, etched in every stained-glass window, stamped on every fixture, carved in every piece of wood. Both pulpit and open Bible give testimony to His word, which is, a *lamp unto our feet and a light unto our pathway* (Ps. 119:105). The baptistry signifies our entrance into the family of the royal priesthood, what Paul calls a *peculiar people. Everyone who calls on the name of the Lord shall be saved,"* so he writes in the 10th chapter of Rome.

The table at the altar is the Lord's Table upon which we place bread and wine. Etched across that table are the words, *This Do in Remembrance of Me* (Luke 22:19). There is no doubt that the lights hanging from the vaulted ceiling, decorated with the cross, speak of God's glory, for God is the light of the world. The vaulted ceiling proclaims that God is God of time and space, and speaks of God's transcendence. The center aisle leading to the altar speaks of God's accessibility and reminds us that we all are priests and that, in the words of the hymn writer, there is *nothing between my soul and my Savior.*

"Of course," you say, "this is the Lord's house." So, why should there be a need to raise such a seemingly ridiculous question as, "Is the Lord in this place?" "Of course the Lord is in this place," you insist. Yet, I contend that just because it is God's house does not mean God chooses to remain at home when we show up. Or the fact that God may be at home does not necessarily mean that God chooses to be bothered with His guests, with our empty rituals, our vain repetitions or our celebration of self.

There is a difference between worship and performance; between being the church and playing church; between the praise of God and the entertainment of self; between prayer that is addressed to God and prayer that seeks to impress others; between songs that celebrate our own musical skills and songs that celebrate the power and majesty of God; between bragging about what *we* have done and remembering what *God* has done.

Notice the song of Moses and Miriam, found in the 15th chapter of the book of Exodus. There is no mention of the Israelites' performance, no mention of their skill in parting the Red Sea, and no mention of their expertise in handling pharaoh. There is no mention of their military prowess against the grinding chariots and snorting horses and shining spears and military hardware of pharaoh's army. There is no mention of how they had to climb up the rough side of the mountain, as if there is any other side upon which to climb, other than the rough side.

No, this song, in Exodus, is all about God, this song is a grand recital of what God has done. Look how often we hear words referring to God, as opposed to the word, *I* and *my*. Listen:

> *I will sing to the Lord, for He has triumphed gloriously; horse and rider He has thrown into the sea. The Lord is my strength and my might, and He has become my salvation. I will exalt Him. The Lord is a warrior. The Lord is His name. In the greatness of your majesty, you overthrew your adversaries; you sent out your fury . . . You blew with your wind, the sea covered them . . . Who is like you, O Lord? Majestic in holiness, awesome in splendor, doing wonders? You stretched out your right hand, the earth swallowed them . . . You brought them in and planted them on the mountain of your own possession, the place that you made your abode, the sanctuary that your hands have established* (Ex. 15).

Then Miriam could not contain herself any longer. *Sing unto the Lord*, she shouted, *for He has triumphed gloriously. Horse and rider he has thrown into the sea* (Ex. 15:21). You see, worship ought to be about more than *me*. Again, I ask the question: "Is the Lord in this place?"

The answer to that question largely depends on the answer to the previous question, "What's going on?" When God sees us coming, is He excited about seeing us? Or is it like some guests who come to your house. They knock on the door. They are strangers, even though we know them. We really do not care whether they come in because the last time they were in the house, they had no respect or reverence for the house or its owner. They thought they were doing the owner a favor by showing up, even acted like they themselves were the owners. They left some money, but it was only a tip, not a tithe. They walked around in the house at inappropriate times, and had no respect for the furniture. They came late and left early, and did all the talking. You were glad to see them go because, even though they left early, it was not soon enough.

Will God say to us, as Amos describes in the Day of the Lord?

I hate, I despise your festivals, and I take no delight in your solemn assemblies. Even though you offer me your burnt offerings and grain offerings, I will not accept them; and the offerings of well-being of your fatted animals, I will not look upon. Take away from me the noise of your songs, I will not listen to the melody of your harps. But let justice roll down like waters, and righteousness like an overflowing stream (Amos 5:21-24).

I ask again, "What's going on?" What happens between introit and benediction, between the beginning of worship and the end, between prelude and postlude, between our entrance into the sanctuary and our departure from the sanctuary that can empower us as God's children? What is it that puts flesh upon dry bones? What is it that makes the wind blow and breathe into lifeless bodies the wonderful breath of the living God? What happens when wind and fire get together in the midst of the holy presence?

When we come to church to dig deep into the well of worship, where we find living water to quench our thirst, what tools do we have at our disposal so that we can glimpse God's glory? How do we move from the shallow waters of worship into deep waters?

There was some good theology in the statement made by the woman who encountered Jesus at Jacob's well. Said she, *Sir, the well is deep, and you have nothing to draw with*

(John 4:11). A mere bucket is not necessary for shallow water. "What's going on?"

While this may be a strange title, this lecture is, *The Romance of Worship*. Yet, I propose that the encounter with God in worship is a kind of *romantic* encounter. If the term *romance* offends us, it is because we see it only in human terms, and even then, we see it negatively. Complicating the problem is that we live in a day of physical love without romance. This modern day divorce between sex and romance shows up in our music and in our songs. There is sex in our music, but no romance. Listen to the words of many modern secular songs, the songs of this generation that reduce human relationships to its lowest common denominator. Notice many lyrics dripping with filth and profanity. Of course, you know that one can be profane without using profanity. Listen to the words of many popular songs of this generation that glorify violence and celebrate self-indulgence, songs that are full of anger and hostility, written and sung by angry young men and women. Listen to words that dehumanize women and celebrate sexual prowess; songs reflecting an *Esau* mentality and songs that will sell a birthright to satisfy an appetite for some beef stew.

When I was growing up, not all, but many songs described that wonderful human encounter between male and female. There was romance in the song, a kind of encounter that spoke of a yearning, a desire for one's lover. There was stage-setting in these encounters, a boy-meets-girl adventure, a kind of mysterious prelude-interlude, a thirst and hunger for love, a wooing of the lover; a chase. There was a sense of wonder and mystery. And when there was a physical and emotional distance that separated lover from lover, love letters would drip with poetic pronouncements of what it's been like since you've been gone, and what it will be like when the geographical barrier is lifted and we see each other face to face and greet with tender embrace. There were the tender whispers over the phone, moments when time stood still and the glow of romantic adventure kept one warm on a cold and chilly night. That's romance.

I submit that on a higher level, the encounter that takes place in worship between God and humanity is a kind of romantic encounter. Perhaps this is why the Song of Solomon (Song of Songs) found its way into the cannon. It is a celebration of romantic love. Or, *As the hart panteth after the water brooks, so panteth my soul after thee, O God* (Ps. 42:1). Romance involves anticipation, wonder, and mystery. It involves a journey through celestial realms where the sky is blue, the sunrise is dazzling, the sunset is bathed in bright orange splendor, the waters are clear, the streams teem with trout, and the mountains are robed in majesty. It involves a love that goes beyond the superficial, that takes us into realms never before fathomed. God is a great lover. My predecessor at Monumental, the Rev. M. M. Peace, would always begin his stirring prayers by addressing God, "Oh, thou great lover of our souls . . ." St. Augustine of Hippo picks up this theme of the love encounter with God. I quote,

> *To fall in love with God is the greatest of all romances. To seek Him is the greatest of all adventures. To find Him is the greatest human achievement.*

We worship God with our hearts, as well as with our heads. To bring the head and leave the heart at home is just as self-defeating as to bring the heart and leave the head. No head, and our worship becomes an exhibition in unbridled emotion, a religious free-for-all, a spiritual exercise in self-indulgence, a wild party where the honoree slips out the back door, while the guests do not know he's gone, and do not care. No heart, and our worship becomes a futile exercise in cerebral speculations about God, a recitation of our opinions about God, rather than our affirmation of our faith in God.

No heart, and our worship becomes cold, stale, formal, sedate and empty of feeling. Take away the heart and you take away the romance. We will wind up knowing how to eloquently recite the 23rd psalm, but will never encounter the Shepherd of the psalm. It's one thing to know the psalm. It's quite another to know the Shepherd.

No heart, and our worship becomes an icebox, rather than a fire burning in the fireplace of the soul. No heart, and our worship becomes only an intellectual exercise, and like the sad commentary concerning the church at Sardis, *You have a name of being alive, but you are dead* (Rev. 3:1). Head and heart must be kept in balance. *Thou shalt love the Lord thy God with all thy heart, and with all thy soul, and with all thy mind* (Matt. 22:37). There is something wrong with a religion that expresses itself only in our hands and feet, but not in our hearts and heads.

The worship of God involves a *touching*. The Greek word *proskuneo* describes this sense that in worship we bow down and kiss God's hand, we touch God, encountering the Lord through personal contact with the Almighty. It is through the worship experience that we encounter this awesome God, who loved us before we knew ourselves. What happens in this wonderful journey that takes place on Sunday morning, this journey that we call the worship service? "What's going on?"

First of all, what happens during the worship service, during this romantic encounter with God, must be seen in light of what happens *before* the worship service begins. The worship service itself is not the totality of the worship encounter. The romantic adventure does not wait until Sunday morning to commence. I know that it is unfair to always compare our ways to the ways of our fore parents, who lived in a different time when the church was more at the center of community life. But, there are some specifics of their journey, which can be helpful as we travel our journey.

One of which is that there seemed to have been, in their time, a greater sense of God's presence beyond the church grounds, beyond the church walls. There was a sense of the holy presence that reached into every corner of their lives. Our ancestors believed that if God is in the sanctuary, God is also in the home. Prayer in the sanctuary presupposes prayer in the home and prayer in the home presupposes prayer in the sanctuary. Their romance with God began in the places where they lived, worked and played. It was in the fields, under the hot sun. In fact, the church was out in the fields before it was ever in a building. Praise was out of doors before it ever came indoors. Our ancestors worshipped in portable sanctuaries, wilderness tabernacles. "I've got a telephone in my bosom," they sang.

There was Bible reading in the home, periods of devotions and praise. Hymns were hummed while chores were being completed. Prayer was always recited before meals and as a result, there may not have been much money in the bank, but there was food on the table. Many of us were raised in traditions where we would dare not begin our meals without each person at the table reciting a Bible verse. And we had better not recite the same verse as another brother or sister. There was no escape. There was a sense of utter dependence upon the grace of God. There were two worship tools in every home: a Bible and a hymnal.

Even today, if you think about it long enough, you can strain your ears to hear in the distance the favorite songs of the ancestors, who no longer walk among us, but who left for us a faith that will not shrink and an old time religion that is both old and new at the same time.

I woke up this morning with my mind stayed Jesus, they sang.

Nobody but you Lord, nobody but you, they sang.
Come by here, my Lord, come by here, they sang.
Fix me, Jesus, fix me, they sang.

This romantic preparation, the romantic prelude, is an essential ingredient in effective worship. When an organist plays the prelude, he or she is establishing the tempo for worship, creating a mood, and setting the stage for the singing of the song. Choir rehearsal is a good place for romantic prelude. The encounter with the Eternal God should not begin in the choir stand on Sunday morning, but in the choir rehearsal room on Thursday night. Just think what a difference it would make if God could get into some of our choir rehearsals. Just think if choir members could, for a moment, stop jockeying for position, influence, and power. Just think if choir members could, for a moment, stop competing over who will sing the solo. Just think if choir members, for a moment, come together and offer the Lord one song. Just think if choir members could, for a moment, forget about their performance and focus on the God who gives us the song.

Just think if the ten choirs in one church could, for a moment, come together and sing to the glory of God, with one voice. If the pastor, worship leader, choir, musicians could, for a moment, sing the same tune, in the same sanctuary, in the same key, to the same God, for the same purpose. What a difference it would make on Sunday morning. Because what happens before worship begins, affects what happens after worship begins.

Let us look briefly at the order of worship. "What's going on?" In the moments between introit and benediction, God wants to meet us. How does the order of the worship service enhance or inhibit this encounter? Why does the choir process? What is the purpose of the introit? Why do we have a call to worship? Why is it important for the worshipper to remain for the benediction?

Three components of worship, which serve as the anchors in the worship service are: Preaching, singing, and praying. There are points in the worship service where the preached word, the sung word, and prayer merge. In other words,

Strange Fire

there is some music in our preaching and in our prayers. There is some preaching in our praying and some prayer in our preaching. Music is richly embedded into our African-American tradition. We have taken seriously the African saying, *Where there is no music, the Spirit will not come.*

In our tradition as black Christians, there developed something called the *Amen corner*. Now, the *Amen corner* was not just a special section of the church where people gathered to say Amen. The *Amen corner* was made up of lay musicians and singers, mostly women, who would tune the preacher into the preacher's key. To those observing from a different cultural perspective, it may have seemed disrespectful to start singing and moaning while the preacher is preaching. But, the Amen corner was the preacher's support group, his backup group. Somebody in the *Amen corner* would start moaning, "Come here Jesus, we need you now," while the others would join in the response. If the preacher struggled a bit to find his key, he would cup his hand around his ear, while somebody would intone, "Help him, Lord." Today, in many churches, the organ does what the Amen corner did in generations past.

There are points in African-American worship where word, prayer, and song are wedded into one grand symphony of praise. Even the announcement period has not been spared from our *call and response* tradition.

We are a responsorial people. We even respond to bad sermons and feel cheated if the sermon is too short. We love to hear the same old story in the sermon, song, and prayer. Our prayers contain rituals. Can't many of you recall the old deacon's prayer, while down on his knees as he thanked the Lord that last night's slumber was not in death, and that the bed he had slept on was not his cooling board, and that the cover he was wrapped in was not his winding sheet?

The power of the Holy Spirit is at work not only in the story, but also, in the telling of the story. A preacher in the black church dare not tell the story of the crucifixion without including some important details. He or she dare not finish the story before the story finished. We feel cheated if we don't hear the word, *early* . . . By that time, song has taken over the sermon and the real celebration begins. This is black worship, and who says we are not a liturgical people? It is an honored tradition, a legitimate liturgical expression of people of African descent. We need not be ashamed of who we are.

Yet, there are some things we need to know about the appropriateness, the meaning, the message, and most of all, the content of what goes on in the space we call God's sanctuary, during the worship hour. For instance, the purpose of the introit is to bring us into oneness of spirit through musical expression. It is a musical call to worship, a melody sounded so that the congregation may know that we are entering the courts of the Lord with praise. It sounds the note of readiness for worship. When the introit starts, everything else stops. It is a reminder that the place on which we now stand is holy ground, however, everybody does not know they are standing on holy ground. Moses did not even know it until he was told. "Moses, I know you grew up in Pharaoh's palace, but take off your shoes, you are standing on sacred ground, and I can't talk to you with your shoes on." We must let others know that they are standing on holy ground. We have got to tell them to stop talking, stop walking around, stop disrespecting the Lord's house and to stop treating the sanctuary like it's a pool hall. Tell them to take of their shoes; they are standing on holy ground.

The procession of the choir dates to the temple worship, and many references are made to the practice in Old Testament worship and liturgy. Today, the choir procession represents the procession of the entire congregation. In the procession the choir is symbolically standing in for the congregation. The prayer response is the choir's *Amen* to what the minister has requested on behalf of the people. The hymns of praise should be sung enthusiastically with the congregation standing. If the hymns are dead, it is because the people who sing them are dead. Do you recall what Jesus said about the dead burying the dead? Congregational hymn singing is almost a lost art in the black church. We allow the choir to do all of the singing, with their special arrangements and contemporary songs that people may enjoy, but in which the congregation cannot always participate.

This spectator worship is not the kind of worship pleasing to God. Congregational singing is in the intensive care unit, breathing its last breath. Let's go back to the hymnal and resurrect those hymns of our faith, and sing them with life, spirit, and joy. Lift the rafters singing, *Come, Thou Fount of Every Blessing; O, For a Thousand Tongues to Sing; Jesus is All the World to Me; Since Jesus Came Into My Heart; My Faith Looks Up to Thee; More Love to Thee, Oh Christ.*

The worship service is composed of different types of prayers, each designed to express on behalf of the people, particular concerns directed to God. Sunday worship consists of at least the following prayers: the invocation, the offertory prayer, the pastoral prayer or, as it is often referred to, the altar call, and the benediction, which is also a prayer, as well as other types of prayers.

The important questions are, "What is it this prayer is supposed to do, or express? What are we asking God to do? If we are the sender and the God is the receiver, what is it the sender wants the receiver to do? Is it a legitimate request? For instance, the invocation would not be offered at the end of service, no more that the benediction pronounced at the beginning of service. The invocation is a prayer inviting the worshipper into the Holy presence, as God also invites us into His presence. It is both a plea for God to hear us, and an invitation for us to encounter God. Remember, it is God's house. In a sense, we are God's guests. The prayer is not so much a prayer for the Lord to *stop by*, but a prayer for God not to leave, to abide with us.

The prayer for the offering is a prayer that God will accept, not just our money, but also, the larger gift of ourselves. It is a request for the Almighty to take control of our resources, our time, our talents, our loyalty, and our tithes. So, you see, to pray that God will *bless those who gave and those who had nothing to give* is a weak prayer. Who is it that has nothing to give? If God has me, he also has my pocketbook, my resources, my commitment, my time, and my energy. The offering is not a time for recess, but a time of excitement and joy. It's time to give. "Praise the Lord!" is the people's response. The offertory prayer, therefore, is not a prayer for the sick, the lame, the blind, the deaf, or the dying.

The benediction is a prayer not to be taken lightly. To miss the benediction is to miss the blessing. It is a prayer of blessing, placing us in the hands of the everlasting God until we meet again. It is a prayer that the Lord will guide, direct, protect, and empower. It is a prayer that puts us in God's *protective custody,* so that, in the words of our ancestors, "No hurt, harm, or danger" will befall us. In our physical absence, the benediction keeps us in spiritual fellowship with one another. Absent, but together. Far, but near. Away from the building, but yet in God's presence.

The Lord bless you and keep you; the Lord make His face to shine upon you, and be gracious unto you. The Lord lift up His countenance upon you, and give you peace (Num. 6:24).

And now unto Him who is able to keep you from falling, and to present you faultless before the presence of His glory, with exceeding joy, to the only wise God, our Savior, be glory majesty, dominion and power, both now and ever. Amen (Jude 1:24).

The issue is not only whether the congregation is listening, but also, whether God is listening. Our God is a God who likes to hear our praise, for God is a jealous God who will not share His glory with another. "Moses, tell the people that I am a jealous God." *Thou shalt have no other gods before me* (Ex. 20:3).

One cannot separate music from romance. Could we worship without a song? Even in dawning of creation, the morning stars sang together and the children of God shouted for joy. Worship is what takes place when the members of the orchestra come out on stage, each with his or her own instrument, violins and flutes, oboes and piccolos, trumpets and trombones, French horns and English horns, each practicing and tuning his or her own instrument. But, when the conductor steps on stage, all eyes are on one person. They play their instruments when the conductor says play. They watch the conductor's signals; they move from cacophony of sound to a symphony of praise. That's music. That's romance. How can we not sing?

When the children of Israel arrived on the other side of the Red Sea, they sang. When the angel broke the news to Mary that she would bear a son and call His name Jesus, she sang. When Jesus and His fearful disciples left the upper room and headed out into the night toward the Garden of Gethsemane, they sang. When Paul and Silas were locked up in a Philippian jailhouse, while other prisoners cursed and complained, they prayed and sang praises unto God.

Why sing? We sing because the kingdoms of this world are on a collision course with the kingdom of our Lord and of HIs Christ, and He shall reign forever and ever.

Why sing? We sing because God is stronger in weakness than man in his strength.

Why sing? We sing because God is able to bring from what was, what will be.

Why sing? We sing because *The earth is the Lord's and the fullness thereof, the world and they that dwell therein. For He hath founded it upon the seas and established it upon the floods* Ps. 24:1).

Why sing? We sing because *He gives power to the faint; and to them that have no might He increaseth strength. Even the youths shall faint and be weary. But they that wait upon the Lord* . . . (Isa. 40:31-31).

Why sing? We sing because *I waited patiently for the Lord, and He inclined unto me and heard my cry. He brought me up also out of a horrible pit, out of the miry clay, and set my feet upon a rock and established my goings. And He hath put a new song in my mouth, even praise unto our God* (Ps. 40:1-3).

Why sing? We sing because *In the time of trouble, He will hide me in His pavilion.*

Why sing? We sing because *God is our refuge and strength, a very present help in trouble* . . . (Ps. 46:1)

Why sing? We sing because, in the words of the hymn writer, *There is a fountain filled with blood* . . .

Why sing? We sing because of what the Lord IS. *The Lord is my shepherd; I shall not want* . . . (Ps. 23:1)

Why sing? We sing because *The Lord is my rock and fortress.*

Why sing? We sing because *The Lord is good, His mercy is everlasting, and His truth endureth to all generations* . . . (Ps. 100:5)

Why sing? We sing because *The Lord is my light and my salvation. Whom shall I fear? The Lord is the strength of my life. Of whom shall I be afraid* (Ps. 27:1)?

Why sing? *I sing because I'm happy; I sing because I'm free*, His eye is on the sparrow, and I know he watches me . . .

Chapter Six
NO NIGHT THERE

Now we turn, in this final lecture, to the Christian funeral. My purpose here is not to discuss the grief process from a professional point of view. Neither is my task to raise issues of death and dying from the viewpoint of the psychologist, or as an expert in the field of pastoral care, though I am a pastor. My task is to look at the matter of death and dying within the context of the Christian funeral and in the larger context of Christian worship. I wish to argue that whatever else the funeral is, it is, or should be, primarily a worship experience. When viewed as such, it can take on new meaning, and lead us into new and exciting directions.

It would be a good idea for pastor and church to come together in teaching and training sessions dealing with the matter of death and the funeral. Death in the congregation should not be the only time we talk about death. A funeral manual could be developed, which can help the people of God understand the theology of the funeral, as well as offer guidelines for procedures to follow. The music ministry might want to look at the music used in the context of the funeral, and reflect upon the theological significance of what our songs say about death and our hope in Christ.

I need not offer any proof that we will die. Is there anyone who wishes to argue with the reality of death? Is there any fighter who has enough power to give death a knockout punch? Is there any running back who can avoid death's tenacious and certain grip? Is there any wrestler who can pin death to the mat? Is there any runner who can beat death to the finish line? Is there any philosopher who can win a debate against death? Is there any grammarian who would dare erase death's period and replace it with a question mark? It's a waste of time to argue the point of death. It does not matter how much we question the meaning of death; it is an exercise in futility to argue the certainty of death.

Since the Bible is a book of real people living in real circumstances it is not surprising that there is real treatment of death. Death is not swept under the rug. Death is neither fantasized nor romanticized. Death is not sugarcoated. Our Biblical heroes do not get to ride off into the sunset, except maybe Enoch and Elijah. They live and then they die. Their deaths are described in simple strokes of the pen, as only the poet can do, for the scientist cannot tread on holy ground. Holy ground is reserved for those who walk with God.

Look at the record. *These are the days of the years of Abraham's life, a hundred and seventy-five years. Abraham breathed his last and died in a good old age, an old man and full of years, and was gathered to his people* (Genesis 25:7-9).

Keep turning the pages. *When Jacob finished charging his sons, he drew up his feet into the bed, and breathed his last, and was gathered to his people* (Genesis 49:33).

Keep turning the pages. *Then Joseph took an oath of the sons of Israel, saying, God will visit you, and you shall carry up my bones from here. So Joseph died, being a hundred and ten years old; and they embalmed him, and he was put in a coffin in Egypt* Genesis (50:25-26). We also see that God's promises were not cancelled even as the heirs of the promise fell asleep. God's promises are always *to be continued*.

Keep turning the pages. *So Moses, the servant of the Lord, died there in the land of Moab, according to the word of the Lord. And he buried him in a valley in the land of Moab . . . but no man knoweth of his sepulcher unto this day. And Moses was a hundred and twenty years old when he died; his eye was not dim, nor his natural force abated* (Deuteronomy 34:5-7).

Keep turning the pages. *Then David slept with his fathers, and was buried in the city of David* (1 Kings 2:10).

The Bible is astonishingly real in its portraits of our sacred heroes. We see them without make-up; we see their warts, blemishes, their failings and follies, their sinfulness and wretchedness. No press agent or publicist can whitewash his or her shortcomings. No biographer can ever wipe away the ugly stains of life.

Who can forget the incident in the life of David (1 Sam. 21), who finds himself in the camp of Israel's perennial enemy, the Philistines? The Philistines remember that this is the man who had killed Goliath their hero. David, out of fear, pretends to be crazy, reasoning that if they think he's out of his mind, they will leave him alone. From adultery to murder, from greed to lust, from conspiracy to deception, it's all there. When it was all over, David died. That is because our heroes die; the saints die. From Abraham, the father of the faithful, who set out searching for a city with the same contractor and architect, all the way to David, the man after God's own heart, they all died; even Sarah and Hagar; Rachael and Leah; and Rahab and Ruth, they all died.

The way we view death has changed through the last two or three generations. There was a time in our society when death was closer to us. Homes were made up of extended families, perhaps three generations living under the same roof or at least in the same geographical area. Before the days of extended care facilities, nursing homes and hospitals, relatives were cared for and eventually died at home. After death, the body was laid out in the home and washed by family members. What we call the *wake* was held in the home where friends came by to pay their respects. Cemeteries were located on or near the family church ground. You could hardly approach the church without seeing the ancestral burial ground–holy ground–a constant reminder of the reality of death.

Today, we have distanced ourselves from death and the dying. Our loved ones die in hospitals or nursing homes. Once they die we may not even see them until they are *laid out* in a mortuary for inspection. The more *natural* they look, the more we fool ourselves into believing that they are just asleep, for the mortician's job is to make the dead look like the living. Our vaults and airtight caskets reflect our modern preoccupation with the preservation of the body, even though the Bible keeps reminding us that we came from dust, and that the nature of grass is that it withers, and the flowers fade. Have we not heard the words of the apostle Paul? *I tell you this brethren: flesh and blood cannot inherit the kingdom of God, nor does the perishable inherit the imperishable* (1 Cor. 15:50).

There was a time, especially in the South, when people stood in respectful silence and men took off their hats when the funeral procession passed by. Now, angry motorists blow their horns, and roll down their windows cursing and swearing because of the inconvenience of having to wait a few moments. Many won't wait, and cut in the line, disrupting the funeral procession.

Today, the funeral itself is viewed by many as an unnecessary ritual, and they wonder why this unnecessary service is permitted at all. Why not just go straight to the cemetery, deposit the body and go back to business as usual? This position seems to be another form of denial of death, and to treat it as if it is of no consequence. We affirm birth, yet want to deny death. We even celebrate the anticipation of birth with baby showers. We celebrate new life through baptism, christenings, and dedications. We recognize the journey's beginning, but want to ignore the journey's end. We stand, facing the east, watching the blazing glory of the sunrise. Yet, we turn our backs to the west, and fail to behold the dazzling splendor of a golden sunset.

The funeral has meaning when given theological content, and when viewed as an opportunity to worship the God who stands at both the beginning and the end of life's journey. The funeral service is not just for the dead, neither is it just for the living. It is for the glory of God. It can give us a peek into the mind and heart of God. It can afford us the opportunity to say to those who will listen, *There is No Night There*.

Having said this, every pastor knows that the funeral has also the possibilities of drama and family tension on a grand scale. The funeral pulls together clashing and colliding human forces and emotions. The death of a loved one can bring out the best and worst in human nature. It brings together members whose relationships may already be strained, family members who may have had no dealings with each other for many years, and who have carried around with them the old beat-up baggage of resentment and jealousy over past grievances that happened so long ago, until everybody else has forgotten what it is, except them. Here they come, each claiming the right to have some say-so in the arrangements. Each armed with a variety of weapons aimed at anybody who gets in the way. Each wanting control and influence. Each desiring to do in death, what was ignored in life.

Then there are those who hang around to see what they can get. In their own minds they have already divided up the inheritance and the furniture. Sometimes it can get very ugly, especially considering that they are arguing and fussing over something they themselves did not earn in the first place. It seems that the very ones who want to make decisions and have the influence are not the ones who are paying the funeral bills.

We all have dealt with people who want to use the funeral as a means of making up for something left undone in the past. Often they act out of a sense of guilt rather than love, and try to make up in death what they failed to do in life. They try to impress us by how much money they put in the ground. They give their money to the florist, even though flowers fade, rather than giving it to the scholarship fund in the church where it can do some good for a struggling student, and where their name can be attached to something that lasts beyond fading flowers, withering grass and a decaying corpse.

Into this mix, the preacher/pastor must stand with a word from the Lord. To be sure, there are those who do not want to hear a word from the Lord, those who do not want to hear anything from anybody, those who do not care. We are all too familiar with the non-church crowd; the crowd who only shows up for weddings and funerals; the crowd who has no respect for God, for the church or the preacher; the crowd who cannot sit still through the service. They do not know our hymns and do not respect our sanctuaries. These are they that just show up to view the remains. There are some people who just seem attracted to the dead.

You remember the man in the Scripture who lived at an unusual address? He was the resident of a place where no mail is delivered. He took up residence in the graveyard. His neighbors were the bleached bones of the dead, housed in whitewashed tombs. No children laughed and played on his street. No schools, shops, playgrounds, and churches could be seen in his neighborhood. He could not go next door and borrow a cup of sugar, nor smell the aroma of food cooking in his neighbor's kitchen. No one on his block made any plans. No one planned for the future. When Jesus asked him, *What is your name?* he must have responded, "I'm a little of *this* and a little of *that*. Not much of anything. My name is Legion."

Then again, if you are dead spiritually and mentally, if you are not going anywhere, you may as well hang around your own kind. If one is spiritually dead, one might as well be physically dead. Adam did not die when he died. Adam died when he sinned against God. There are people who will go to funerals to view the dead, but will not go to church to learn more about a man who said, *I have come that ye might have life, and have it more abundantly* (John 10:10).

There is a crowd that will tell us to make the eulogy *short and sweet*. What they are really saying is to *cut the God-talk*. The singers can sing all day. The reading of the cards and telegrams can take all day. By the way, the funeral service is neither the time nor the place to read every resolution and sympathy card. The "mini eulogies" of the dead by friends and acquaintances can take all day. But, the sermon, the message, with the words of life, the "God-talk," the living water is hardly valued.

One of the problems of our day is that we're asking the wrong questions. The Bible tells us which questions to ask, therefore, which questions that beg for an answer. "Is there a word from the Lord?" That's a good question, even if no one but the preacher raises it; even if the preacher stands alone in the asking. Noah did not build an ark after taking an opinion poll to see whether or not it was a popular idea. God's ambassadors must raise issues of life and death on God's behalf. God's questions must be raised and answered. "Yes, there is a word from the Lord." A word of hope, joy, peace, a word of life, a word of salvation. Brother, sister, you can change your address. You can move out of the graveyard, out from among the tombs, and leave a forwarding address. How can the funeral service be used to enhance the worship of God, to show forth who God is and how much he cares for His children?

First of all, the funeral service belongs to the church, not to the family. Therefore, all of the family's wishes and requests cannot and need not be honored, especially if those requests are contrary to our Biblical and theological understanding of worship. Again, let's emphasize that the funeral is also worship, a particular form of worship, but worship, nonetheless. This does not mean that it should be turned into an evangelistic service, even though sermon and song may have evangelistic overtones. It is not revival. It is a funeral service within the context of worship.

The time and day of the funeral service is not arranged by the mortician or by the family, but by the pastor and the church. The pastor is not the last to be notified, but the first. The order of service should follow the outline established by the church. It always amazed me how the people who have the least amount of time for the church, give the least to the church, do not even go to church, are usually the ones who make the greatest demands on the church's time and resources.

The pastor is in charge of the funeral service, and should never feel the need to apologize to anybody, including another preacher, for presiding over and preaching in one's own pulpit. He or she is neither obligated nor should feel pressured to defer to anyone or honor any request from the family that someone else preach the funeral or that someone who knew the deceased since childhood should say final words. It is the pastor's prerogative to stand where the pastor has been called to stand, and to do what he or she has been called to do. The pastor may, out of courtesy, allow another to stand in the pulpit, but that choice is the pastor's alone.

The funeral service is not merely a celebration of the life of a person, but it is a celebration of God as reflected in the life of a person, assuming the person's life is, indeed, a reflection of God's glory. That's why one cannot eulogize everybody, because one cannot always say something good about everybody. It amazes me how much of a tendency there is to exaggerate truth in death. The worst sinners become saints when the obituary is written. Death seems to transform a lukewarm Christian into a dedicated believer. All of a sudden the dead become the best members ever to belong to the church.

It happens all the time when our obituaries outdistance our living and our resumes bear no resemblance to our works. It's a good thing that God does not read our obituaries. Rather, it is God who writes our obituaries. In the words of the Negro spiritual, *My Lord is writin' all the time.*

Too often the funeral service is used by the family to put themselves and the body of the deceased, on exhibit. To leave the casket open during the service or to reopen it after the eulogy puts the emphasis in the wrong place. The purpose of the funeral is not to put the body on display, for death is not the focus. This is not a denial of the reality of death, but an affirmation of life in Jesus Christ.

This brings us to the music of the service. If, indeed, the funeral is worship, the music and the songs must lift the worshipper beyond the low ground of sorrow and despair, and proclaim, in song, what the preacher proclaims in sermon that, *There is no night there.* Guidance and direction must be given to the family, and the church and its leadership must be educated and trained in the matter of death, dying, and the funeral. Too often our songs have more syrup than substance, more sentimentality than theology. We sing the same old tired refrains, sentimental favorites, or even the top ten on the funeral hit parade. We bow to family requests. Rather, we should seek to lift the spirits of the worshipper through congregational singing that is alive, spirited, and celebrative.

Higher Ground . . . A Mighty Fortress is Our God . . . On Christ the Solid Rock I Stand . . . O, God Our Help in Ages Past . . . Blessed Assurance, Jesus is Mine . . . 'Tis So Sweet to Trust in Jesus . . . All the Way My Savior Leads Me . . . All Hail the Power of Jesus' Name . . .

It is advisable that the casket be closed before the service of worship begins and kept closed. Help does not come from the casket. *I will lift up mine eyes unto the hills . . .* (Ps. 121:1-2) We must be careful what kind of punctuation mark and accent are used here. The text accurately reads: *I will lift up mine eyes unto the hills!* and *From whence cometh my help?* Therefore, the text makes a declaration, followed by a question. *I will lift up mine eyes unto the hills!* The question is: *From whence cometh my help?* Or *from where will my help come?* The answer is: *My help cometh from the Lord who made heaven and earth.*

For the believer, the funeral service does not place a period at the end of life's sentence. There is something else; another punctuation mark. God is always changing our human syntax, rearranging the sentence structure. It makes all the difference in the world how one structures the sentence. The theme of the funeral, therefore, the theme of the music and song, ought not to be death, but resurrection; not defeat, but victory; not tragedy, but triumph; not the terrestrial, but the celestial; not human strength, but God's power. Do you not know that God's weakness is stronger than man's strength? And since God is stronger than death, *There is no night there.*

Look at the baby born in Bethlehem on a calm, silent night, while Caesar sat on his throne and legions of soldiers stood at attention, ready to defend the empire with military might and lethal power. We have a weak, helpless baby, just fresh from His mother's womb, crying for some milk, lying in a manger. This child could not defend Himself because He was weak and helpless. But to save humanity, God risked being made vulnerable in the form of an infant. And look at Him about 33 years later, dying on a Roman cross on a hill called Calvary. He was, again, weak, helpless, tired, and thirsty. Death had our savior by the throat. Listen to Him cry out in agony and pain, *My God, my God, why have you forsaken me* (Mat. 27:46)?

If we look at the New Testament record, we will find that death was never really highlighted. Whenever death appears, so does Jesus. When the ruler of the synagogue came and knelt before Him saying, "My daughter has just died," Jesus did not rush. In fact, he took time to speak words of comfort to a woman who had suffered from twelve years of hemorrhaging, giving comfort to her, saying, *Daughter, be of good cheer; your faith has made you well* (Matt. 9:22). He then had the nerve to tell the distraught father of the dead girl, *She is not dead, she's just sleeping* (Mat. 9:24).

A funeral procession was winding its way through the bumpy road through a little village called Nain, just south of Capernaum, where a mother was taking her only son to the cemetery for burial. She must have been thinking about the bills due, and the fact that a woman without a husband or a son would have a tough time. The world in which she lived had little compassion for widows and orphans. Well, look who's standing at the gate of the city. Jesus touched the hearse and said, *Young man, I say you, arise* (Luke 7:14). He then gave the son back to his grateful mother.

Mary and Martha of Bethany send word to Jesus that Lazarus, their brother, is sick. When Jesus heard it, he sent back a message, *This sickness is not unto death, but for the glory of God, that the Son of God may be glorified through it* (John 11:4). By the time Jesus finally reaches Bethany, Lazarus had been dead four days. *Lord, if you had been here, my brother would not have died* (John 11:21), said Martha. "Martha, what does it matter if he's been dead four days or four months, since I am the resurrection and the life?"

That's the problem. We have turned the funeral service into a celebration of death. My question is, "Why give death more press coverage than Jesus gave it? Why give death such a platform? Why?" Death gets enough attention on the evening news. Once the evening news begins, how long is it before the spotlight is focused on death? Look at the headlines of the morning newspaper. How many articles in the average daily newspaper focus on death? It seems that death punctuates every page. The more blood and violence, the more death seems to command our attention. Everywhere one turns death hovers overhead like a brooding shadow. Name one teenager who has not had at least one friend or acquaintance claimed by death, usually in a violent manner. It seems

to me that someone ought to stand in the holy place and shout from the rooftops, *There is no night there.*
There is night every place else, but no night there. You see, night is more than just night. Night has theological significance. Night signifies spiritual blindness. Night is the blindness of any soul not knowing who Jesus is. Night is to not understand the matters of the spirit. So, Nicodemus came to Jesus by night. Not clock time, but spirit time. And Jesus said to him, *Are you a master of Israel, and knowest not these things* (John 3:10).

Jesus said to His disciples, *But if a man walk in the night, he stumbleth, because there is no light in him* (John 11:9). When Jesus and His disciples huddled together in the upper room, He said to Judas, *Whatever thou doest, do quickly.* (John 13:27). Judas immediately went out, and the Scripture says, *and it was night.*

Launch out into the deep and let down your nets for a catch, Jesus says to His disciples as they fished in the Sea of Tiberius. *Master, we have toiled all the night, and have taken nothing* (Luke 5:5).

All night catching nothing. Night and nothing? What a futile combination. Night plus nothing is a hopeless combination. Dangerous, until Jesus stopped by. I would not want to come to the end of my journey and all I have to show for my struggle is night plus nothing. Jesus said, *I must work the works of Him who has sent me while it is day; night cometh when no one can work* (John 9:4).

Night, with its brooding shadow and somber skies. Night, a symphony written in a minor key; a bright fantasia turned into a melancholy melody. Night, when owls hoot and wolves howl. Night, when the baby's temperatures rises. Night, when the sun is veiled behind a thick curtain and an eerie mist covers the deep.

Night, when hair turns gray, and steps are short, and eyes grow dim, ears strain to hear, memory fades, flesh decays,

No Night There

and death's shadow draws nigh. Somebody needs to stand up and say, "There is no night there. There may be night down here, but there is no night there."

John said, "I'll tell you what I saw. I saw a river, clear as crystal, proceeding from the throne of God. I saw a tree with twelve manners of fruit, and the leaves of that tree were for the healing nations." But, *there was no night there. . . . and they need no candle, neither light of the sun; for the Lord God giveth them light: and they shall reign forever and ever* (Rev. 22:5).

When the night is over . . .
When the mist has rolled away.
When the trumpet shall sound, and the dead in Christ shall rise.
When the morning comes. We shall understand it better, by and by.
When we shall behold Him, face to face.
When they crown Him King of Kings and Lord of Lords . . .

Chapter Seven
A DAY IN THY COURTS

James White, in his book, *Introduction to Christian Worship*, reminds us that worship takes place within the context of time and space. Indeed, our worship is a response to a God who acts and is revealed in time and space. Revelation, too, occurs at that intersection where time is invaded by eternity. The work of creation began at that moment when God said, "Let there be light," and there was light. Incarnation takes place at that moment in time when God chose to enter the human bloodstream through the person and work of Jesus, who is the Christ. The significance of time for the Christian is that, *the word was made flesh, and dwelt among us* (John 1:14). The apostle Paul, in writing to the Galatian church, explains,

> *But, when the fullness of the time was come, God sent forth His son, made of a woman, made under the law, to redeem them that were under the law, that we might receive the adoption of sons* (Galatians 4:4-5).

The writer of Hebrews opens his missive with a statement of God's activity in time, in the person of Jesus, the Christ.

> *God, who at various times and in various ways spoke in time past unto the fathers by the prophets, has in these last days spoken unto us by His Son, whom he hath appointed heir of all things, through whom also He made the worlds* . . . (Hebrews 1:1-2).

Our worship is a celebration of an event that took place, and continues to take place, in time, namely, the Christ event. We gather in worship to give praise to the One who is both in time and above time, and without whom time would have no meaning. We gather on a particular day in time, namely Sunday. Originally, the early Christians gathered each Sunday to celebrate the Resurrection of the Lord from the dead. Therefore, for those early Christians the day of His Resurrection became the Lord's Day. The Biblical concept of time is not *chronos*, but *kairos*. *Chronos* is clock time. *Kairos* is God's time, given meaning by the revelation of God in human history. Throughout the year the church highlights different aspects of God's revelation in Christ. Even in so-called non-liturgical traditions it is important to pay attention to the church calendar, as it relates to events in the life of Christ and His church, and what we believe concerning the meaning and message of those events. This does not suggest that in the black church, we become slaves to the church year, and locked into pre-planned themes.

However, we must keep in mind that we are always in competition with the secular calendar, and the people to whom we minister live, as we do, in a secular world. In the world of business, Monday is the first day of the week, not Sunday. People plan vacations and other events based upon the *secular year*, with its emphasis on human activity, rather than as response to divine activity. Therefore, we must always keep in view what God has done and continues to do in time. There is a difference between Memorial Day, as holiday, and Good Friday, as holy day. The people of God must be made aware that we do not wait until Christmas Sunday for worship to focus on Incarnation, but that prior to Christmas Sunday the four Sundays in Advent constitute a season of preparation and expectancy, as we *anticipate,* through word and song, the birth of God's Son. What a great opportunity we have throughout the year to preach on the great themes of our faith. When the church calendar becomes important to us, at least two things will happen. First, our worship will avoid becoming stale and monotonous. Second, it forces us to accept the challenge of dealing with themes, that, for one reason or another, we may tend to avoid. The Christian calendar consists of at least the following seasons: Advent, Christmas, Epiphany, Lent, Easter, Pentecost, and Trinity, to name a few. Other special days, such as Father's Day, Mother's Day, and Children's Day, have been culturally incorporated into our religious life. These special days, though not exclusively secular, are not strictly speaking Biblical, even though they may have been inspired by Biblical themes. However, care must be taken so that, for instance, Mother's Day does not become an occasion for over-sentimentality, or a subtle form of idolatry. Remember, Mother's Day is still the Lord's Day. We must be careful that these special days do not go too far in making our own cultural traditions the main focus of our worship. Perhaps the Biblical importance of the family as it relates to the transmission of faith, is a more appropriate focus. At its best, worship, therefore all of life, is shaped by the saving events of the life and ministry of Jesus, rather than around our national holidays.

Since Martin Luther King's birthday is a national holiday, even more attention has been drawn to the social justice themes of freedom, justice, and equality. However, the church does not take its cues from the state. The church, and particularly the black church, has historically preached the gospel of social justice and equality, which is firmly rooted in Biblical faith. The exodus event was, in fact, the beginning of the pilgrimage of God's chosen people. Therefore, these social justice themes of deliverance from oppression and injustice are at the heart of the Biblical message. What an opportune time to emphasize God's mighty acts, particularly the act of deliverance. It is at this point where the song of Miriam comes alive:

And Miriam answered them, Sing ye to the Lord, for He hath triumphed gloriously; the horse and his rider hath He thrown into the sea (Exodus 15:21).

At the heart of Jesus' trial sermon in the synagogue is a concern for social justice. He turns to the book of Isaiah and applies these words to Himself:

The spirit of the Lord is on me, because he has anointed me to preach good news to the poor. He has sent me to proclaim freedom for the prisoners and recovery of sight to the blind, to release the oppressed, to proclaim the year of the Lord's favor (Luke 4:18-19).

There has been some discussion in recent years concerning the appropriate hour of worship, and many churches have adjusted the time of worship to meet the needs of the congregation. Surely, 11:00 am is not necessarily a more sacred hour than any other. In fact, the church has in the past adapted the time of worship to meet the needs of the worshippers. Many churches have at least two worship services on Sunday morning. A generation or two ago, in the black church, Sunday evening worship was necessary since many blacks worked in homes on Sunday, but were able to attend Sunday evening services. In our urban centers, evening worship for various reasons is less popular today, especially since many church members live a distance from the church. Earlier worship services on Sunday, as well as Saturday worship services, have become popular in many churches today. There is a sense in which ministry in the church must be flexible, and not carved in stone.

However, we must guard against the notion that worship is just a footnote, a mere appendage to our schedules. We must not approach the hour of worship as if it is an intrusion, therefore, let's *get it over with*, so we can get to other things. Worship is not something we merely *fit in*to our schedules. Worship ought to be the believer's greatest desire. The psalmist gives worship its proper place in the life of the believer.

One thing have I desired of the Lord, that will I seek after: that I may dwell in the house of the Lord all the days of my life, to behold the beauty of the Lord, and to inquire in His temple (Psalm 27:4).

Just as worship takes place in time, it also takes place within the context of space. The writers of the Old Testament wrestled with the paradox of a God who is both beyond and within space. Yet, they saw God as the Eternal who, because God chooses, can be located in space. In dedicating the temple, Solomon raises the searching question:

But, will God indeed dwell on the earth? Behold, heaven and the highest heaven cannot contain thee; how much less this house which I have built!
(1 Kings 8:27).

The church sanctuary is the *space* in which we gather for worship. That space may be a gothic cathedral, with its flying buttresses, a wood frame building on the side of a rural road, or a storefront in the heart of the inner city. It is still the space for the gathering of God's people. It is *sacred space*. It is still a house of worship. What does the space in which we worship say about God and about us? Even more important than the space in which we worship is the question of what's going on in the space. British architect Norman Foster writes that, "architecture is an expression of values." If it is also true that architecture is the organization of space, we need to look at how we use this worship space. Space for a football stadium is organized in the best possible way, not merely for the players on the field, but for the spectators, those who will witness the sporting event. The event itself influences the organization of the space where the event takes place. The needs of both players and spectators are of primary importance. How sanctuary space is organized is vital to the worship of God.

For a congregation considering construction of a new church edifice, or extensive renovation of a present one, the selection of an architect is of vital importance. Here, a distinction must be made between a church architect and an architect who designs church buildings along with other buildings, but sees no difference in the two. An architect who builds churches may simply design church buildings in the same manner he or she would design a factory or a supermarket.

However, a church architect seeks to clothe theological concepts with meaningful forms, shapes, and spaces for the people of God. This becomes a ministry in itself. Even though we have tended to overuse the word *ministry*, there is a sense in which what we do should be done to the glory of God, even the building and design of God's house, becoming a *service*, indeed an *offering* to God. This is not to say that a *Christian* architect is necessarily more qualified to build church buildings, just as a *Christian* physician is no more qualified to treat illness and disease then one who is not Christian. An architect who claims no religious faith, whatsoever, may in fact, be more faithful to the theological vision of God's people. The important factor is that the architect must grapple with and grasp the faith of the congregation in such a way that gives flesh and bone to spiritual ideas. When it comes to the building and design of a church, the twofold question becomes, "How shall it look?" and "What is its function?"

To take the matter a step further, what does a person mean by the statement, "Oh, that doesn't look like a church."? What does a church look like? When does contemporary become faddish? How is the congregation's place in the community defined? What will be the theological emphasis? What is the church's witness in the world? Will the building resemble more the space age, or the God of the space age? However, these questions are answered, the building wherein we worship must reflect theological integrity. American architect Edward Sovick comments on the matter by saying that, "Those who erect structures which are taken to be the symbols of the Christian community, should commit themselves to the forms which are faithful to the Christian vision." Not only does the architect inform the congregation, but also, the congregation informs the architect through its own understanding of the theological traditions of the faith. The architect listens, interprets, and guides, using his or her skills, training, and expertise, to give shape to and help sharpen the congregation's vision.

We must be careful at this point to be sure of what the church really is. A cross on a building does not alone make the building a house of worship. Religious activities, alone, do not make a church. Naming a building a church does not guarantee that God has taken up residence inside. In this age of upheaval and urban change, we have all seen church buildings sold and turned into apartments, restaurants, or commercial space. Many are boarded up as ragged remains of past glory, where, once upon a time, beautiful stained glass reflected the sun's soft rays. The rafters no longer ring with the thunderous sounds of *Holy, Holy, Holy*.

During the author's seminary days, the officials of the school took the gym and, with surprisingly minor changes, transformed it into the chapel. How, and at what point, does "gymnasium" become sanctuary? When does "building" become "church"? The same brick, mortar, or stone used in the building of churches is used in the construction of prisons and factories. Stained glass is also used in restaurants and homes. Consecrating pews does not necessarily mean that persons who sit therein live consecrated lives. The answer lies in purpose and mission. *Christian architecture*, then, it is the organization by God's people of God's space to do God's will. Buildings may burn, but the church is still the church. Christian architecture articulates the vision of God's people in form, function, and space. Hardly ever did I hear my father call the church building, the church. He called it the *church house*.

Since God is holy, the place where God's people worship ought to be holy also. Biblical faith bears testimony that God is holy. Moses was instructed to take off his shoes, for he was standing on holy ground. This is *desert theophany*, at its best. The truth is that, in reality, the secular has sacred potential. The church does not blend in with the world around it. Rather, by the power of God, the church defines and transforms the world so that it, too, reflects the glory of the divine. The men and women of the Old Testament, in particular, were always careful to mark the spots where they encountered the divine presence. Ordinary ground became holy real estate. However, the holy ground, on which Moses stood, would have no meaning whatsoever, and his encounter with the divine would have blown away in the dust of the Midian Desert, had he not responded to the God of Israel beckoning him back to Egypt to demand the release of his people.

What, then, is the importance of architecture? Its importance lies in how it speaks to us about God. Where the building is located, what it looks like, how it is landscaped, how easy or difficult it is to enter, what color is the exterior, all say something about the congregation's beliefs about God. The vaulted ceiling, the arches, and slope of the roof, say something about who God is. The narthex, the color of the exterior walls, the windows, which shut out distractions, while allowing the light of God to peek in, all speak of God's majesty, mystery, and glory. Whatever else the building is, it ought to be a place of beauty and warmth, which has little to do with the cost of the structure or the size of the sanctuary. Whether the sanctuary is small or large, it must speak of the mystery, majesty, and nearness of God. To this end, the pastor and church building or renovation committee would be wise to engage the most capable and skilled architects and builders.

We now turn to a discussion of church buildings sold and bought by congregations of other denominations. Many black congregations, particularly in urban areas in the North, have purchased church buildings and synagogues previously owned by other congregations, whose theology and faith may have been different from theirs. Consequently, many congregations have been limited in their quest for buildings that speak to their faith traditions. In spite of some obvious limitations and restrictions, it may be possible, with minor changes, to bring the design and layout in line with the theological suppositions of the new occupants. The basic design of most church sanctuaries is the style of the *basilica*, a rectangular Roman law court, with space for the audience, and a platform for the judge. This type of structure prevailed and continued. Our sanctuaries, basically, include space for the audience (congregation) and the judge (clergy). Space for the choir, the Lord's Table, the offering table, and Baptism, are also included.

Let us look more closely at these worship spaces. First, is congregation space, or *nave*. In worship, audience becomes congregation. The people of God are not mere spectators, but participants in the drama of worship. Congregational seating should allow for a feeling of closeness between pulpit and pew. Many modern sanctuaries are designed to widen, rather than lengthen the space between pew and pulpit. This brings people in the rear closer. Many sanctuaries built in the 19th and early 20th centuries were of a *horseshoe* design, with seating that uses side and balcony space. Seating should be comfortable with a reasonable amount of space between pews. Any respectable church pew company will see to it.

The pews should be well stocked with an adequate supply of hymnals, that is to say, in churches where hymnals are still in use, for the presence of hymnals can be a visible and strong symbol of who we are as people of God. The importance of the hymnal should not be minimized, for the songbook is a compilation of songs and tunes containing the church's theology. Today, many churches use modern technology to show the words of songs on large screens, making the hymnal, as we have known it, almost obsolete. Bibles, also, have been a staple of the pew in many churches, until recent years. Though technology has made the Bible available on our smart phones, there is something to be said to seeing worshippers coming to church with Bible in hand. Both hymnals and Bibles are important living symbols of our faith and identity.

Now a word about the space called the pulpit. By pulpit, we are referring to the elevated platform area, even though *pulpit* also refers to the *desk* or podium from which the minister preaches, as well as the elevated platform. The elevated pulpit serves two purposes. First, it allows the congregation a better view of those who lead worship. It is also important that the congregation's view of those who lead is unobstructed. The presence of posts and columns, though in many cases necessary, hinder the worshipper's view. Second, and more importantly, it says, theologically, that the Word of God transcends us. The Word is above us, but not so high as to be beyond our reach. Isaiah's vision of God in the temple is helpful. The eighth century prophet from Jerusalem describes God as, *high and lifted up* (Isaiah 6:1). I do not agree with many who seek to reduce the pulpit to *pew level*. There are those who want to erase the line between congregation and pulpit. It might be added that the one scriptural reference to pulpit is in the book of Nehemiah:

> *And Ezra, the scribe, stood upon a pulpit of wood, which they had made for the purpose . . .*

And Ezra opened the book in the sight of all the people (for he was above the people) (Neh. 8:4-5).

The Hebrew word, *mighdal*, or pulpit, means a *high place*. Jesus preached and taught from *high places*. The pulpit, then, is a physical representation of a spiritual truth. It is a symbol of God's presence and transcendence that God is both with us and above us. The design of the pulpit area bears witness to the beliefs, practices, yes, the theology of the congregation. Many church sanctuaries are designed with a divided chancel, meaning that the Word is preached from the side of the platform, and the altar is in the center, reflecting, architecturally, the doctrines and beliefs of that particular congregation. Congregations, which have bought church buildings not reflecting their own theology, must either leave the design of the pulpit the way it is, or find a way to renovate and center the pulpit so that it reflects their understanding of the importance of and primacy of the preaching of the Word.

Historically, preaching has been central in the black church tradition. Worshippers gather to hear the preacher *tell the story*. For most African-American worshippers, it is not just the content of the story, but the re-telling of the story, an old story that takes on wings each time the preacher mounts the pulpit. Preaching in the black religious experience is pastoral care at its best, in that it addresses the brokenness and hurt within the congregation with the healing power of the Gospel. Especially is this true in black congregations where worshippers have been stung historically by oppression and racism. The great early 20th century American preacher, Harry Emerson Fosdick, called preaching, *personal counseling on a group basis*. In the black church, preaching, the salvation of souls, and transformed lives, are the foci of worship, and the congregation is actively involved in the preaching moment. There is no *altar,* per se, although in many black churches the *altar call* is the moment in worship when the congregation gathers in the front of the sanctuary, as the preacher speaks to God on their behalf. In this tradition the Communion Table, or the Table of the Lord, is in front of, and lower than, the pulpit, and is too important a symbol of black church theology to be moved to the side or hidden from view, only to be brought out when used. The Communion Table needs to be always visible and in its rightful place in the sanctuary.

Preaching involves communication and communication involves hearing. In order to respond to the Gospel, the Gospel must be heard. For preaching or speaking to be effective, the sound system must be adequate and the acoustics conducive for sound to travel effectively to the listener. Often the microphones in the choir space are of better quality than the microphones on the pulpit. Much care and thought should be given to a church's sound system. Experts tell us that the shape of the sanctuary, carpet, draperies, and furnishings, all affect the quality of sound. The sound system is an extremely important investment, and is crucial to effective worship.

Choir space is needed, also, in most sanctuaries, unless, of course, music is not a component of worship. The choir is usually located behind or to the side of the pulpit space, facing and in full view of the congregation. The placement of the choir may also reflect the beliefs and doctrines of the congregation in the same way as the placement of the pulpit. There were times in the history of the church when the choir loft was elevated and behind the congregation, hidden from the view of the worshippers, so that the singers were to be heard, but not seen. If the choir is also congregation, and the singers are themselves worshippers themselves, then the position of the choir space mirrors this belief.

The choir is, in fact, part of the congregation; participant, as well as song leader. Often, this point is forgotten, as the choir members may view themselves as entertaining the worshipper, rather than a part of the worshipping congregation. The disadvantage of choir space located behind the pulpit, is that the singers cannot see the preacher's face. Also, unnecessary movement and excessive talking can serve as easy distractions. Choir robes have been worn for centuries, and if choir robing is a part of the church's tradition, care should be taken in the selection of the robe, so that, liturgically, the robes compliment the worship space.

Along with choir space is space for the placement of instruments, most notably, the organ and piano. Often, little thought is given to the position and placement of the organ, which is still the main instrument used in many churches, to accompanying the song. Obviously, the organ should not be located behind the choir, or with the organist's back to the choir, or on the opposite side of where the choir sings, especially in churches where the organist is also director. If the director is also the organist, it is important that the choir see the him or her without difficulty, so that direction and guidance can be given with a minimum of effort. In many churches, the choir still depends upon the organist/pianist for direction.

A musical instrument itself is neither religious, nor irreligious, neither sacred, nor secular. There were times in history of the church, when both organ and piano were resisted as a secular invasion of the sacred. An organ is no more a religious instrument than a drum or a trumpet. Having said that, it must also be stated that any instrument can be misused. At issue for some, is not the use of instruments, such as drums in contemporary worship, but their misuse. Instruments should not be used to evoke artificial emotion and *packaged* responses. Even the organ should not be used to provide *mood music* and *play over* the worship service from beginning to end, as syrup poured over pancakes. Much thought should be given to the placement of instruments in the sanctuary.

Baptismal space is another space requirement. Again, the preferred form of baptism is a reflection of the theology of the particular church. Even though denominations differ on form, method, and meaning, baptism for all Christians is entrance into the family of God through Jesus Christ, and occupies a central place in our theology and practice. Like the Passover meal, baptism has Jewish roots. It was used in the Old Testament as an act of cleansing. It is believed that the Essenes, a Jewish religious sect, existing during the time of Jesus, practiced baptism. John the Baptist preached a baptism of repentance as a prerequisite for entrance into the new age that had begun to dawn. The baptism of Jesus by John in the river Jordan is the centerpiece of our belief in baptism, and is an event recorded in all three synoptic gospels, (Mark 1:9-12; Matthew 3:13-17; Luke 3:21-23). Scholars tell us that Ephesians 5:14 contains fragments of an early baptismal hymn, with its reference to *sleep* and *death*, which speak of the condition of the soul, and awakening into new life. There are many examples of hymn and hymn fragments referring to baptism in the New Testament.

In the black church, baptism is not only a symbol of repentance and new life in Christ, but acceptance into the family of God as well. This is quite important to those in an earlier time who had been disconnected from family members during slavery, or later those who migrated *up north* to find better jobs and escape the nightmare of segregation and discrimination. The presence and location of the baptismal pool or basin, in the sanctuary, is of great importance. As stated earlier, in many cities, black congregations have purchased church buildings representing different theological influences, as seen in their architectural design. Many sanctuaries bought by congregations where baptism by immersion is practiced were not equipped with baptismal pools in the sanctuary. Therefore, these churches have had to carve out baptismal space, either in the sanctuary or somewhere else in the building. Whatever the case, baptism must be seen as one of the most significant events in the life of the congregation.

One item seen in most churches across the country is the American flag. Flags, ensigns, and banners have been used for centuries, by nations and individuals, as badges and symbols of culture, and were used in ancient times by the Egyptians and Assyrians. Flags have been used to lead armies in war, and if the soldier carrying the flag in battle were stricken, another would rush to keep the flag from falling. Perhaps Numbers 2:10 is a reference to the flag or banner as a symbol and sign of identification with the clan and tribe. It is the writer's contention that the American flag, a symbol of patriotism and national pride, is inappropriate in the sanctuary of our God. We, as people of God, must not confuse patriotic zeal with religious faith, faith that often demands that we choose between God and country; between the Cross and the flag. We bow at the foot of the Cross. The Cross is always in conflict with the decaying kingdoms of this world.

The writer suggests, in the absence of documentation, that the American flag began to appear in church sanctuaries during World War II, to foster national pride and patriotism during a very challenging time in our history when the American way of life was threatened. Congress passed laws encouraging the flying of the flag in and around government buildings, schools, and places of public assembly. Since worship services were, at the very least, *public assemblies*, the American flag became a common fixture in sanctuaries and church halls across the country. Presently there are laws determining the placement of a flag over a casket, its ranking when flown among other flags, and its positioning on a platform. There are also rules governing how it is to be raised, lowered and carried.

The Christian flag began to appear in church sanctuaries in the early decades of the 20th century, perhaps as a way of giving balance in the worship space, as if God needed defending in God's own house. However, the presence of the Christian flag seems counterproductive, since, according to the US flag code, the positioning of the American flag in public buildings always defines the positioning of other flags.

The code states that the American flag must be positioned on the platform to the right of the speaker, and no other flag should be flown higher than the American flag. Therefore, even the Christian flag must assume an inferior position to the American flag.

The church of Jesus Christ must always stand in prophetic judgment over the state. To use the great theologian H. Richard Niebuhr's typology, Christ is not the Christ in culture, but the Christ who transforms culture. Creative tension must always exist between church and state. To remove the American flag from the sanctuary is not unpatriotic or disloyal to country. Rather, it is to recognize that the flag has no place among the sacred symbols of the faith, for we must affirm the Lordship of the Christ who transcends geographical boundaries and national and ethnic loyalties.

In the very beginning of this book a scripture appears, taken from Paul's first letter to the Christians in Corinth, as the great apostle to the Gentiles gives instructions concerning worship. For at the very center of our worship–as well as worship in the early church–is the celebration of the Resurrection of our Lord. As stated earlier in this presentation, when it comes to worship, it is important for us to *get it right*. Paul wants the Christians in Corinth to, *get it right*, he therefore, proceeds to spend the balance of chapters 11 thru 13 trying to help these often stubborn Corinthians to *get it right*. Since we know that chapter and verse divisions in the Bible came later, it makes sense to connect the chapters, especially chapters 12 and 13, as Paul ends chapter 12 by saying, *And now I will show you a more excellent way* . . .

In our day, as in Paul's, we must be careful not to allow our worship to become a tool of the devil, who is always seeking to derail us. What better way for the devil to sneak into our midst than through our worship? The great reformer Martin Luther says it best: *Next to the Word of God, the noble art of music is the greatest treasure in the world.* As we sing the Lord's song, we must be careful not to play the devil's music–which has nothing to do with our misguided debate between the sacred and the secular–and by doing so, prevent Christ from being where He must be, which is always at the center of our music and our worship.

When in our Music God is Glorified
Lyrics by Fred Pratt Green
When in our music God is glorified,
and adoration leaves no room for pride,
it is as though the whole creation cried,
Alleluia!

How often, making music, we have found
a new dimension in the world of sound,
as worship moved us to a more profound
Alleluia!

So has the Church, in liturgy and song,
in faith and love, through centuries of wrong,
borne witness to the truth in every tongue,
Alleluia!

And did not Jesus sing a psalm that night
when utmost evil strove against the Light?
Then let us sing, for whom he won the fight,
Alleluia!

Let every instrument be tuned for praise!
Let all rejoice who have a voice to raise!
And may God give us faith to sing always,
Alleluia! Amen.

ABOUT THE AUTHOR

J. Wendell Mapson, Jr., was born in West Palm Beach, FL and raised in Newark, NJ. He received his Bachelor of Arts degree from Morehouse College, Atlanta, GA., a Master of Divinity degree from Crozer Theological Seminary, Chester, PA. (now Colgate Rochester Crozer Divinity School, Rochester, NY.), and a Doctor of Ministry degree from Eastern Baptist Theological Seminary, Philadelphia, PA. (now Palmer Theological Seminary). In 2002, Palmer conferred upon him the honorary Doctor of Divinity degree. He has served as an adjunct faculty member at both Palmer and Lutheran Theological Seminary in Philadelphia, and lectured and taught at other institutions of higher learning.

From 1969 to 1987 Mapson was pastor of Union Baptist Church, Elizabeth, NJ, and in July 1987 he was called to the historic Monumental Baptist Church, Philadelphia, one of the oldest black Baptist congregations in America, organized in 1826. He is now serving as the pastor with the second longest tenure in the church's 190-year-old history.

Dr. Mapson is highly sought after as a preacher, and has lectured extensively in the area of music and worship in churches and colleges across America. He is the author of *The Ministry of Music in the Black Church* (published, 1984), considered an early authoritative work addressing issues of worship and music in the black church. It is still used in seminary and college classes, as well as by pastors, church musicians, and choirs seeking to understand music and worship from a Biblical perspective. He is also author of the more recently published, *God of My Father: Sermons of a Father and Son*, a collection of sermons of his father (deceased) and himself. In 1994, he was inducted into the Martin Luther King, Jr. Board of Preachers at Morehouse College. Mapson has been a featured lecturer at the prestigious Hampton University Ministers' Conference, and instructor for the Choir and Organists' Guild. He is a past president of the Baptist Pastors' and Ministers' Conference of Philadelphia and Vicinity, and a member of Alpha Phi Alpha Fraternity, Inc.

He is married to Shirley Jones Mapson, and they are the parents of three sons, Keith, Brian, and Jesse III.

CPSIA information can be obtained
at www.ICGtesting.com
Printed in the USA
BVHW040635110921
616582BV00014B/398